THE DANISH
SECRETS OF HAPPINESS

HYGGE

HOW TO BE HAPPY AND HEALTHY
IN YOUR DAILY LIFE

MAYA THORESEN

Download The Audio Version Of This Book Free!

If you love listening to audiobooks on-the-go or enjoy the narration as you read along, I have great news for you. You can download the audio book version of

SCANDINAVIAN LIVING TIPS WITH HYGGE AND LAGOM DIY BUNDLE

for FREE just by signing up for a FREE 30-day audible trial. Just scan or use the links below:

For Audible UK:

https://tinyurl.com/y45l9ncr

For Audible US:

https://tinyurl.com/y4sald4h

HYGGE

The Danish Secrets of Happiness: How to Be Happy and Healthy in Your Daily Life

Maya Thoresen

© 2017

Contents

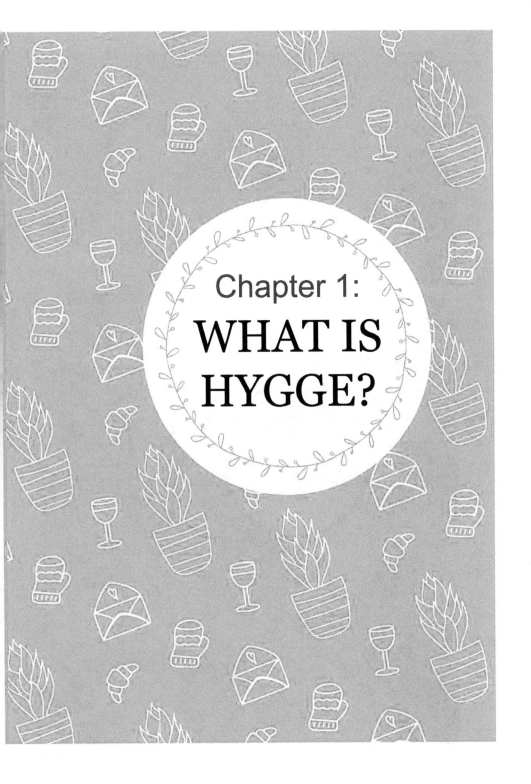

Chapter 1:

WHAT IS HYGGE?

Have you ever heard of hygge? This word is synonymous with coziness and comfort, but many people are currently unfamiliar with its use. In essence, hygge refers to a concept that is deeply rooted in Danish and Norwegian culture. As it is a cultural norm in Scandinavia, it might explain why people in this area experience a higher quality of living than other cultures. Hygge is linguistically versatile and can be used to refer to all aspects of life in the form of a noun, verb, or adjective.

If you were to ask a Danish person precisely what hygge means, he or she would clarify that it doesn't mean just one concept. Instead, there are numerous elements that comprise this way of living, and you may already be doing some of them unknowingly period. Although there is no true English translation of the word, the best connotations that come to mind when thinking about "hygge" include "cozy," "warm," "contentedness," "comfort," "togetherness," and "relaxation." However, these impressions only begin to skim the surface of a much broader concept.

As far as its practical implications, hygge is extremely useful for self-care as well as tending to both the mind and body in the cold winter months. Many scholars believe that is how the concept began: It made the winter more bearable and comfortable for the early Scandinavians.

Hygge has, however, transformed into a worldwide trend that has been gaining popularity in the last few years because of its simplicity and its adherence to the trend of minimalism. Often, Westerners complain about busy lives in which they never stop moving, so applying hygge concepts to their daily practices can improve their overall lifestyles. By integrating some of the hygge principles into daily routine, one can greatly improve their overall level of happiness.

IS HYGGE A GOOD FIT FOR YOU?

You may find yourself wondering whether or not hygge is the right for you. After all, it might sound difficult to make so many changes in your life at once, or maybe you think you're not the kind of person who can really do something that drastic. But as long as you're looking for a way to reduce clutter and ease your mind a little too, hygge is the perfect fit for you!

Specifically, hygge can work for individuals, couples, families, and anyone who wants to feel better and more mindful of their experiences. Another way to determine whether or not hygge is right for you is to consider what makes someone more receptive to living the hygge way. To contemplate if the hygge lifestyle is right for you, try asking yourself these key questions:

- Am I stressed out by normal, everyday life? **There are many ways to deal with the stress of daily life. For many who give it a try, hygge can help reduce the overall sense of stress and emotional and psychological trouble. Practicing a hygge lifestyle helps you slow down and take everything one step at a time. It also helps you live in the moment and enjoy the time you spend doing the things you love, so you feel more capable of dealing with the things you may not like so much.**

- Do I feel like I need to recharge my mind? **Hygge can be a great way to recharge mentally. Keep in mind that hygge is about staying in the present and practicing mindfulness as much as possible. For this reason, keeping hygge in your heart can enable your mind to feel more rested and recharged more often, too. If you feel overwhelmed all the time by the events and people around you, be sure to take some time for mindfulness as well as self-care. These proactive measures can make a big difference in** improving your feelings daily. They also increase your emotional and mental resilience.

- **Do I have trouble coping with changes or problems?** Both can be scary, and while some people are able to address these situations with dignity and ease, others may lack coping mechanisms, causing stress and panic. If you're someone who isn't sure how to deal with uncertainty or pressure, hygge can assist you. By remaining mindful and taking care of yourself and your feelings, you can use hygge to feel better about problems that may arise. Although you may not be able to completely solve every issue with hygge, it's a great tool to help you feel calmer in the face of adversity.

- **Am I always thinking about money, work, or some other stressful part of my life?** Bring hygge into your finances, your job, your romantic relationship, your family, and any other part of your life that may be causing you to feel overwhelmed. The more you focus on a source of stress—like work, for example—the more it consumes you and keeps you from living your best life. When you allow hygge to influence your life instead, you will be able to work through these kinds of daunting issues more effectively. Hygge can allow you to feel comfortable and safe even when you're dealing with dilemmas and chaos in other aspects of your life.

- **Do I want less clutter?** If so, hygge may be a perfect solution for you. This lifestyle is all about reducing clutter and keeping things as minimal as possible. Although you do not have to give up everything for hygge, you should be willing and able to abandon a little bit here and there to make your life less cluttered and confusing overall. You'll use minimalistic furnishings and items in your home when you live the hygge way, and you won't keep a bunch of unnecessary junk. The more you work on downsizing, the more organized your home and life will become. Engaging in this practice can help you feel calm and more hygge than ever before!

- **Do I feel like I never have a chance to take care of myself?** Self-care is a big part of hygge, so if you're worried about not being able to take care of your own feelings and needs, this lifestyle may work well for you. However, it's important to remember that hygge is not about putting yourself first. Instead, it is about making equal time for yourself and for everyone important in your life, too. Don't neglect your friends and family in favor of your own needs, but don't abandon your own needs either. Finding the right balance will help you feel at ease and will improve your hygge experience.

- Do I value things that are comfortable and cozy? If you love to be physically comfortable and surrounded by things with soft, pleasant textures, hygge is definitely the lifestyle for you. Hygge is about making sure you have both sensory and aesthetic comfort available to you at all times. To illustrate, decorating with soft, comfortable fabrics and gentle lines and textures throughout your home is a major part of hygge– though it's important not to overdo the décor, or spend too much money on it, either. Keep things simple and easy when you decorate, and you'll be able to enjoy that comfort even more in no time.

- Would it be nice to have more time for the things and people I care about? Sometimes, it may feel like you can't make enough time for your friends, your romantic partner, your colleagues, or your kids. No matter what you try to do, does it seem like someone is always excluded from your plans? If you feel this way frequently, you may need to try regrouping with hygge. Hygge can help you organize your time better and make sure everyone you care about is getting an equal share of your energy and time. You can also spend time being comfortable and cozy with the people you care about to improve your hygge experience as well.

Of course, these questions really only start to explore the reasons why you may be interested in hygge. Just keep them in mind while you're trying to figure out whether or not this lifestyle is conducive for you. Hygge is very forgiving, so if you try it and find that it doesn't work for you, there's no reason to feel discouraged or guilty. This attempt just means you haven't found the right lifestyle plan yet, and that's okay!

WHY COZINESS?

What is it about being cozy that makes it such a valuable feeling, and such an integral part of hygge? Coziness helps you feel comfortable and safe. This feeling encourages you to slow down, to consider your experiences and surroundings, and to take time for yourself while also giving your time to others. When you're cozy, you're more likely to be happy, content, and at peace with yourself and the world around you. Practicing hygge will help you increase your coziness in no time.

But is it really that easy to be cozy? Is it beneficial to try practicing such a lifestyle when the world around you is so hectic? Many people believe trying to be cozy and comfortable in all aspects of life is futile. Critics feel that taking too much time to relax will prevent individuals from being ready to face problems and situations that might arise in their day to day lives. These critics insist that hygge practitioners will be unprepared for the twists and turns of life if they're too busy taking care of themselves to pay attention to the stressful world around them.

However, practicing hygge and coziness does not imply that you're unprepared or not paying attention to the world around you. In fact, being cozy and relaxed can help you better face problems when they do arise. In essence, hygge can help make it easier for you to cope when things go badly. The more comfortable you are during the good times, the more rested your brain will be when it needs to address problems. You'll also be able to heal emotionally from life's inevitable stresses when you practice a cozy lifestyle, too.

There are many reasons why you might want to incorporate coziness into your life. There's more to it than just being comfortable, and you may be able to find new ways to face life in all its forms when you make hygge a key part of your regular lifestyle.

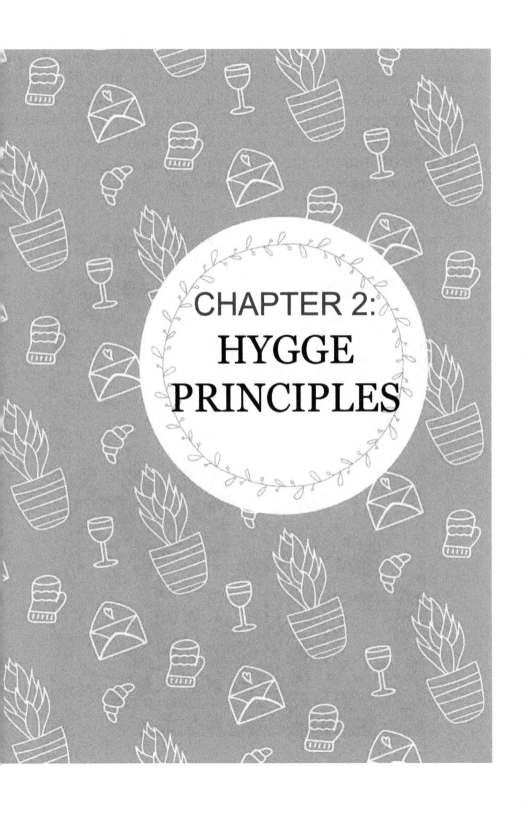

CHAPTER 2:
HYGGE
PRINCIPLES

So far, you have gotten a glimpse of how you can incorporate the Danish way of hygge into your life in diverse ways, all of which you will learn more about throughout this book. The simplest way to begin is by engaging the basic principles of hygge, which are the primary foundations of the lifestyle. Once you grasp these tenets, you will be well on your way to implementing them in your life, and therefore, on your way to improved health and happiness!

1. Mindfulness and the Senses

Mindfulness may be the hardest principle on the list, yet it is one of the most important to cultivate your true happiness through this practice. Mindfulness means you are paying attention to the moment. You are fully engaged in whatever activity you are immersed within presently.

Here are some common situations in which you can practice being more mindful of what you're doing:

- Watching a movie

- Reading a book

- Having a conversation with a friend

- Drinking a cup of tea

Mindfulness refers to any moment in your life where you are absorbed in the moment, enjoying yourself, and not worrying about the past or the future. Think of it as the adage, «Stop and smell the roses!»

In the chaotic and fast-paced modern world, many of us forget to enjoy the moment because we are so busy thinking about that deadline we have to meet or the groceries we have to pick up for the week. Hygge encourages you to change this behavior. Let the aroma of a cup of coffee reach your nose before you take a sip. Enjoy the intricacies and colors of your loved one's eyes, and notice how soft your cotton sweater feels against your skin. Combining your attention without distractions with a full sensory experience helps you slow down the clock and enjoy your time. These seemingly simple moments also help you create cherished memories you can reflect upon later.

Mindfulness is a habit you must develop over time. You can't expect yourself to always be mindful; you have to constantly work on it. One great way to achieve mindfulness is to simply stop what you are doing a minute or two each day and savor the world around you. Take this time to breathe in deeply and truly process what you're seeing, hearing, feeling, and doing. When you are engrossed in a task and realize your mind is wandering, pull it back to the present. Redirect your thoughts to the present moment until it becomes a habit for you to think in this manner.

2.   Gratitude and Being Positive

It may seem like common sense that looking at the positive side of things would make us feel happier, but that doesn't mean it is an easy practice. In fact, we may not even realize that we are being negative sometimes.

The first rule of bringing positivity into your daily life is feeling and expressing gratitude. When was the last time you told someone you appreciate them, or thanked them for opening the door or helping you with the dishes? These are the little things we often forget, and it can make our days brighter because we are making someone else happy when we express gratitude. When we feel grateful for something, we are also feeding on the positive flow of energy from the person we have thanked. A simple show of thanks can go a long way, especially if someone has had a horrible day.

The next step in positivity is about finding that bright spot in the darkness. There is no denying that this world is a chaotic one that can sometimes lead to heartache. Fortunately, you can often find something good in your life on which to focus, even in the worst circumstances.

Think and act positively in all you do. Choose to talk about the good things instead of complaining. Look for sources of good news instead of overwhelming yourself and feeling down about all the tragedies around the world. It is important to be informed, but not to the point that you feel depressed due to dark and gloomy headlines. You do not have to think about bad news 24/7 to stay in touch with what's happening globally and locally.

3. Nature

If you know anything about the Nords and their traditions, you saw this one coming. Being active in nature is not only calming but also inspiring. Nature is what we come from, physically and spiritually. Even if modern conveniences make our lives easier, there is still a part within each of us that summons the wild. Nature is a great way to practice using all your senses as well. Smelling flowers, feeling the cold chill of the wind on your cheek, listening to birds singing, and seeing the bright colors of spring can inspire anyone's appreciation and encourage them to love the world around him or her.

It is important to incorporate nature into your life. Here are a few easy suggestions to accomplish this goal:

- Go on a hike.
- Visit the beach.
- Keep potted plants in your home or on your patio.
- Work in the garden.
- Spend time sitting outside, even if you're just relaxing.
- Bring your family members, pets, friends, or colleagues along for these outside excursions.

4.   Ease and Comfort

This is something that can easily be expressed through what you wear or how things are done in your home. One of the words used to describe the word hygge is "cozy," and that is what you are trying to achieve. Surround yourself with things that bring you comfort and warmth.

Try these ideas for keeping things comfortable in your home and in your life:

- Use pillows that are soft, comfortable, and minimalistic, instead of flashy and impractical ones.

- Wear your favorite sweatpants and a comfortable sweater for the day instead of dressing up.

- Go makeup-free when you feel like it.

- Keep soft slippers available for use indoors.

Remember, comfort and ease go hand-in-hand, so the comfortable choices you make should not be challenging or difficult ones.

Choose to abandon the discomforts of life if you can. Of course, you can't always avoid discomfort since it is an inevitable part of life, but sometimes you endure uncomfortable things because you choose to do so. You don't have to! If you have a pair of shoes that look nice but feel horrible, donate. You don't need to sacrifice comfort for temporary beauty.

If there is someone around you who makes you uncomfortable or radiates a negative presence, don't feel as if you have to keep this person in your life. If talking it over doesn't work, it's better to free yourself from that negativity and bad influence, and focus on the people who bring happiness and comfort to your life. You should evaluate people that you don't like or don't want to be around, and remove them if you can.

Making life easier does not make you lazy; it makes you smart. If you find a way to streamline work or automate your technology, then do so. You are busy and tired enough—why add stress to your life by doing things the hard way? Remember, comfort and ease are important factors in your new lifestyle.

5.   Togetherness

The Danish believe in spending quality time with one another. **Friends and loved ones should take up a good portion of your time, even if it feels difficult to make time in your busy schedule. Don't you feel better after a cup of coffee with your best friend or a Netflix night with your spouse? There is a reason for that. We are all connected, and we are all meant to complement one another. You cannot have true happiness without taking advantage of companionship.**

One of the major principles of this time spent with those you care for relates back to mindfulness. It means giving your full attention to the people that you are with currently. Cell phones and other distractions can keep you distant and only allow you to experience part of the moment. These should be set aside in favor of conversations and physical closeness. Stop letting insignificant distractions get in the way of truly being there with your loved ones.

Remember that none of us live forever, so appreciate the people you love while they are still here. **Although this mentality may seem morbid, focus on how you can enjoy your time with loved ones instead of the limitations of time. Be mindful and stay in the moment with them, avoiding both internal and external distractions.**

There are many lesser problems we may face, even without worrying about death. Plenty of us are taught to keep our problems to ourselves. We don't want to burden other people with the things that bother or distress us. We feel like an annoyance when we are upset or have a problem. But hygge encourages you to connect with the people you care for and with those who love you. Part of forging that connection involves reaching out to your family and friends when you need help. Talk to them and share what is bothering you. Form stronger bonds with them by letting them into your life, your mind, and your heart.

You can't deal with life alone, and you will enjoy and appreciate having the support of these people by your side.

6. Pleasure

Hygge is all about enjoying the simple pleasures of life. Can you honestly say that you do that regularly? You may take a vacation or two every year and make time for a fancy date night once a month, but hygge principles actually embody something even simpler than that. Hygge pleasure is about slowing down and enjoying the small things that you don't have to look far to find. This could be your favorite dessert, a walk along the beach with the feeling of sand in between your toes, or the laughter of your children as you tickle them. We need to learn to find these moments and make them happen. Pleasure in a hygge lifestyle is about the experience around us, instead of unexpected lavish gifts and large expensive events.

There are countless enjoyable moments around you all the time, but the majority of us fail to pay attention to them. One of life's little secrets is that the wealth and pleasure you work hard for and wait for is usually not what you expect. You could work relentlessly for a lavish vacation, only to have things go wrong and end up not enjoying the free time. You save up for months to buy that product you want, only to find that it doesn't work as well as you wanted. You work tirelessly at your job to increase your wealth, only to find that years have passed, and you don't have as much time to enjoy the fruits of your labor. When you put a desire on a pedestal and delay life in order to strive for it, it will evade you. It will never fail to disappoint. When you accept pleasure as something that surrounds you and something that you create consistently with your attitude, then you will find that pleasure is much more abundant and available than you think.

Again, pleasure does not require time, money, or other people. It requires a focus in attitude. You must be open to pleasure; you must accept it without trying to change it or control it. You must look for it in the world around you and be grateful for it when you find it. True joy lies in the little moments. Embrace those moments. You will get into the habit of finding them more and more throughout your day when you start to adopt the hygge attitude and lifestyle.

Of course, you don't have to lie back and wait for pleasure to come to you. You can deliberately create a more pleasant atmosphere and situations in your life. Hygge is something that can come naturally, but you can do many things to emphasize it and foster it in your life. If something brings you pleasure, why not add it to your life and boost your mood as a result?

8.   Minimalism and Quiet

Part of hygge is the belief that minimalism will bring you peace and happiness. This mentality applies for every facet of life, but especially in regards to your home décor. Having the bare minimum that you need in furniture with a simple layout, including a quiet corner to have some time alone to read or meditate, can make you feel less cluttered.

Excess amounts of stuff can stress you out and bog down your energy. You have too many things to worry about, organize, and clean. There is no need for so much clutter. Having a more minimal lifestyle allows you to breathe, both literally and metaphorically.

You might consider Swedish death cleaning. This type of cleaning is a decluttering method where you ask yourself, "What do I really need in my life?" It encourages you to remove excess things that you don't need. Consider how your loved ones will have to clean out your house when you pass away. The more unnecessary things you have, the more stress they will have to deal with upon your passing. You can minimize that potential stress by getting rid of the things you can absolutely live without or excesses that you no longer need. Let yourself be freer by omitting clutter.

If you can't let go of something for some sentimental reason, then keep it, but find clever ways to store these things. One option is to invest in a storage unit, put the items away, and give them some time to sit there. After a while of not living with the sentimental items and not seeing them, do you still want them? Or can you safely get rid of them, knowing you won't miss them?

Another tip is to hang your clothes backward. When you wear clothes and put them away again, hang them the right way. At the end of the year, if there are any clothes left that are still facing the wrong way, you know that you never wore them. You can probably get rid of them without regret now.

Consider donating things instead of throwing them away haphazardly. Remember the classic expression, "One man's trash is another man's treasure?" You might just make someone's day by giving him or her something for free or at an affordable price. The act of being kind to others can give you a warm sense of pleasure, which is all part of hygge.

POSSIBLE HYGGE PITFALLS

Although the principles listed above may sound easy, they can be more challenging than you may realize. Be aware of these potential mistakes and pitfalls that could hinder your hygge attempts:

- Spending too much time on yourself. **Although helping yourself feel better and reducing stress in your own life is a big part of hygge, you should also make time for your friends, pets, colleagues, and family members. Hygge is about making yourself comfortable as well as increasing the comfort of those around you. It's also about learning to love yourself and others more, and about expressing that love and appreciation, too.**

- Spending too much money. **You may be tempted to throw out everything you own to replace it with more minimalistic furnishings and items, but that isn't very practical and can make you more stressed and anxious. If you're already trying to practice hygge on a budget, this can be even more upsetting and difficult. Even if you're not on a budget, there's no need to waste the items you already have. Instead, you may want to just remove some of the items in your home while keeping those you can use. Remember that hygge needs to be functional and practical to work.**

- Unrealistic expectations. **Hygge works slowly, over time, to improve your mood and help you feel good. It isn't going to immediately solve all your problems with your job, relationships, or life in general. Go into it expecting to work to achieve those goals, rather than looking for a magical fix. Even with lots of time, hygge may not solve every issue in your life. This concept is not meant to be a quick solution, but rather a lifestyle change that can help you learn to face problems and work through difficulties more easily. Be sure you're approaching hygge with a healthy mindset to get the most out of it.**

Be on the lookout for these pitfalls when you first get started with hygge and later on in your practice, too. These issues can appear at any time throughout your hygge experience, but they can be easily avoided when you're prepared to potentially deal with them. If you're practicing hygge with others in your life, then you can help each other look out for signs of these hazards, too.

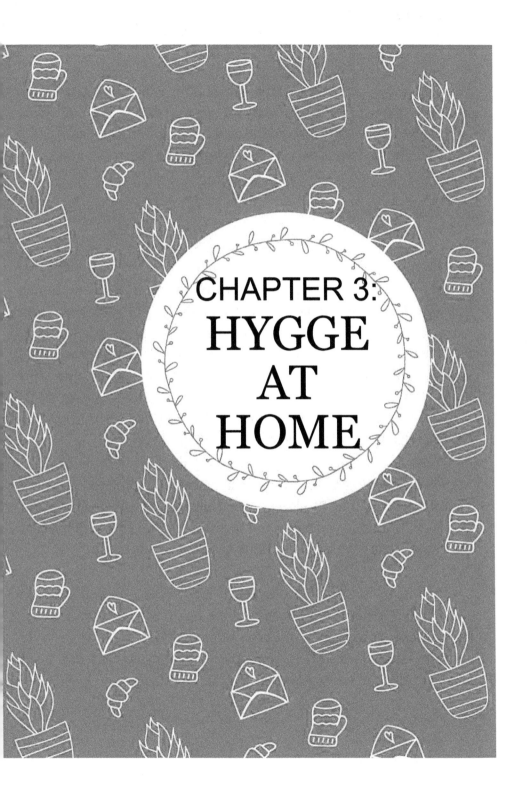

CHAPTER 3:
HYGGE AT HOME

HYGGE – The Danish Secrets of Happiness

Much of the hygge tradition is practiced within the home, so it stands to reason that you would need to change your home, at least a little, to reflect your new lifestyle. Happiness should be centered around the home as a place to relax with your friends and family. It is a precious sanctuary where you can unwind and be your authentic self. All of your worries and stresses need to be left at the door.

HYGGE DÉCOR

Hygge décor is simple. It is easy to incorporate into any home, and the décor itself is aesthetically pleasing. "Minimalism" and "simplicity" are the key terms in gauging how the hygge house should feel. Instead of creating a chaotic home that bogs you down with mess and induces stress with constant organizing and cleaning, try to simplify things. Often the most beautiful homes are designed by simplicity. Ever noticed how homes that are stuffed with things and clashing décor aren't necessarily pleasing to the eye?

At the same time, your home is a place that should bring you pleasure. Therefore, you want it to look a way that appeals to you. You want to fill it with things you enjoy looking at. You want to add items that give your home that special unique quality that says you.

Your home décor should also be useful and functional. A large glass figurine that is easy to break in a home with a lot of activity, for example, is impractical. Useless décor serves to be monetarily wasteful, and you could use that space for items you actually need and can utilize in daily activities.

Let's consider another example: If you love playing pool but find that you don't have room for a pool table because of your fancy coffee table, ask yourself, "Do I ever use that coffee table?" Replace the coffee table with the pool table and rearrange your furniture. Or maybe you have a sofa set with many pieces that makes it difficult to navigate the living room. Why not get rid of the couches you don't use and replace them with things like a bookshelf or a TV that you will actually use?

Go for décor that is simple and functional, preferably in light or warm colors. Pastels or warm colors are more cheerful than dark, depressing colors. Be sure everything that is meant for comfort is comfortable, and make use of texture. You can incorporate texture with pillows, blankets, rugs, and other accessories that make you feel great when you feel them between your fingers and toes. Remember to choose minimal, functional furnishings that feel soft and comfortable whenever possible.

Much of the best décor can be found in places such as Etsy, where many crafty individuals apply their talents and passion to create hygge items and accessories. Handmade items are often more comfortable, have a personal flair to them, and are pleasing to the eye. Plus, they add character to your home.

When it comes to making space in your home, you can go to The Container Store or order cute storage bins and shelves online. Store your stuff out of the way and keep it organized neatly. You can ensure that your storage is both attractive and functional. Having clutter everywhere to trip over is not attractive nor functional. It is far better to put things in proper places, as it will make your home inviting and easier to clean.

HYGGE AND ANIMALS

Did you know you can practice hygge through your pets, too? Pets can offer comfort and are calming. They're also cute. Pets often relieve stress and bring joy to your life. However, it's important to be sure you make the right pet decision for your household and your lifestyle.

For example, a snake may not be the best option if you are afraid of reptiles or do not know how to care for one. On the other hand, if you aren't afraid of them, and if you live in a small apartment or a place where you cannot have a more traditional pet, a snake, lizard,

CHAPTER 3: HYGGE AT HOME

or frog may be perfect for you. A dog may not be ideal if you don't have time and will worry about it too much while you are at work. In contrast, if you have a big family with lots of people who can help care for it, then a dog may be the right choice.

Remember, too, that pets are a responsibility and can sometimes add to your daily stresses. Will you be willing and able to take care of the pet if it gets sick or injured? Would vet bills add to your stress about money? Will you be able to keep the pet for its whole natural lifespan? Consider all aspects of pet ownership before deciding to bring one home.

CREATING A HYGGE ATMOSPHERE

Hygge is all about how you feel, so even if you only have simple and comfortable furniture, this approach is a great start. Fill every room with something that makes you feel cozy. Try Egyptian cotton sheets on your bed, cashmere clothes for relaxing on the sofa, and scents in your bathroom that soothe and heal you, such as lavender. If you surround yourself with little things that make you feel good, you will soon find you are a much happier and healthier person on the inside.

Other items such as a drawing your child made at school, a sentimental treasure from your childhood, or stuffed animals are all things that you can add to each room to bring you that warm fuzzy feeling of being home. Sometimes, it is okay to sacrifice perfection and beauty for comfort. If you have something that doesn't quite match your home's theme, but still makes you happy, then show it off! You will be creating a conversation piece while lightening your mood when you are home.

As mentioned, creating a hygge lifestyle and atmosphere doesn't require you to go out and spend a fortune on new décor, especially if you don't have the budget for it. Any splurging will only increase your stress and defy the basic concept of hygge. Instead, use what you have, or buy small, inexpensive things. If you can, splurge on a few items that you absolutely love so you can have a few high-quality pieces that bring you comfort and joy. Just remember that you don't have to go on a huge shopping spree and spend money you don't have to make your home comfortable.

If your home makes you happy as it currently is, and if it is full of joy and cheer, then perhaps you don't need to change much or even anything at all—it is clearly perfect for your needs. But if your home depresses you, stresses you out, or embarrasses you in some way, it may be time for some changes. Your home environment impacts your mood significantly, so make it something you can enjoy living in and brings you comfort. You will notice an improvement in your life when you change your home to reflect who you truly are and what you like.

THE IMPORTANCE OF CANDLES

Imagine a time before electricity, when heat and light came from fires and candles. Danish winters are bitter cold, and hygge was as much of a necessity as it was something beautiful to hold onto in bleak times. Wrapping up in blankets and gathering around the fire or using candles to illuminate a room to tell stories or enjoy a delicious meal doesn't have to be a practice of the past. The warm glow of a candle, as well as the soothing scents you can find , can work wonders on your mood.

In hygge homes, you will find many candles lit year-round. Using candles is often the first step in creating a new hygge way of living as it is the most iconic piece of the puzzle. You can go with simple tea lights or find a beautiful candle with a scent that makes you feel relaxed. Find pretty candle holders that play with the light in attractive ways. You can also utilize small lamps and natural salt lamps to create a warm, romantic ambiance. The options are endless—it's up to you to discover what you like for your home and lifestyle!

HYGGE IN YOUR PERSONAL SPACE

Hygge is all about creating a personal space where you can leave your cares behind and simply enjoy the act of existing. Part of the hygge lifestyle is creating a personal space where you can become mindful and leave your stress, worry, and pain at the door. Your personal space does not have to be the whole house, especially if you share your house with other people. It can simply be a room or even a corner in a room. It is a small, comfortable space where you can be your authentic self. You can go there to recharge after a long day and engage in your hobbies.

Make your personal space uniquely yours. Decorate it however you want. Common features are pleasing aromas, comfortable furniture, cushy pillows, and lights that make you feel warm and at peace.

Remember that your personal space is just for you. You can expect to be left alone here. Tell others that if you are in your personal space, they should leave you be. Only invite in the people that bring you joy and make you feel good. Toxicity should stay at the door! Because you are using this space for relaxing, try to remove electronics and communication devices from the area. Let this space cradle you and melt away your worries. You don't need to be distracted by work when you are in your space, either. This is a peaceful place, so if you choose to read a book while you're there, choose something easy and light rather than a difficult or sad book.

Remember to use your personal space for what you enjoy doing. A personal space could be a craft room or a yoga studio. It could be a studio where you paint or an office where you write. If you love cooking, it could be your well- stocked kitchen where you create many culinary delights. It could be your man cave, where you watch football and enjoy a beer after work. It could simply be your half of the bed, where you meditate and write in your journal before you go to sleep. Just make sure that this space is functional for what you choose to do with it. No one can tell you what to do in your personal space, because it is yours!

HYGGE MUSIC AND MOVIES

Another great way to keep hygge in your heart at all times is to choose music and movies that give you comfort and joy. Pick music and movies you can enjoy with your loved ones, and if you have kids, choose kid-friendly media as well. Try to select options that can brighten your spirits and help you feel light and free.

For example, stay away from music with violent or upsetting lyrics, and pick soothing, softer songs instead. But don't forget to listen to your favorite bands and singers now and then, too. Even if you love loud rock music, this music can be hygge if you listen to it for the purpose of enjoyment and calming down your busy life for a little while.

While it's better to avoid music with troubling lyrics most of the time, you can listen to it when you're in the right frame of mind. Just don't let this type of music get in the way of your hygge experience, and don't let your children listen to this type of music with you until they are old enough to not let it interfere with their hygge, either.

The same goes for movies. This suggestion doesn't mean that you can never watch movies with heavy themes or upsetting content. Sometimes, these movies can help you learn to better process your own feelings and thoughts within the safe space of a fictional story. In other words, movies like this can sometimes be cathartic. However, it's important to approach this type of movie with the right frame of mind. Don't watch an upsetting or violent movie when you're already feeling emotionally low or unhappy about something. If you have children, don't view these kinds of movies around them, either.

Music and movies don't have to be all happy all the time, and you don't have to surround yourself only with spa-like sounds or documentary-style films to benefit from your entertainment. Just remember, as with everything else, approach the media you enjoy with a hygge mind and never choose movies or music that prevent you from feeling comfortable or cozy.

HYGGE SELF-CARE

There are many ways you can practice hygge self-care. They may be as simple as buying a small, low-cost gift or treat for yourself, or as elaborate as an at-home spa day. Take care of yourself in whichever ways bring you a sense of calm and happiness. Don't overdo it with money, or you may stress about your budget. And don't take so much time for self-care that you forget to spend time with your friends and family, either.

Start small by sprucing up your personal space or setting aside an hour for a bubble bath and some relaxation time. From there, you can look for other methods of self-care you may want to try. Here are a few types of self-care you can practice, ranging from the easy and affordable to the more elaborate:

- Buy a nice bath bomb and take a long, relaxing bath. **Pick one that won't stain your tub, so you don't have to worry about scrubbing it right after you finish your relaxation time.**

- Make yourself a favorite cup of tea and sit under a blanket while you drink it. **Put on some of your favorite music quietly in the background as you sip.**

- Check out a book from the library on a subject of interest. **Take a half hour every day to read it and expand your horizons a little more.**

- Touch something with a texture you enjoy, such as a soft pillow or even a plush toy. **You may also want to try buying a stress relief ball for yourself, so you can have a positive tactile experience during your relax time.**

- Rearrange your personal space a little. You don't have to spend any money to do this, but just use your existing items instead. Move things around so that they're a little more efficient and organized for your hygge experience.

- Treat yourself to a new shirt, pair of pants, or whole outfit. Don't overdo it when it comes to the price tag, but pick something that complements your style and makes you feel good to wear it.

- Treat yourself to a massage or a spa day, but only if you have the time and money to do so. This indulgence is not a requirement to practice hygge self-care, and should only be considered a bonus, so don't over- spend!

CHAPTER 4:
HYGGE AT WORK

Hygge may seem like it has nothing to do with business or work. After all, the very idea of work is often not relaxing or cozy. Instead, work calls to mind the image of agonizingly long days and lots of stress, which is a common work environment for most Americans and Europeans. Longer work hours make a healthy work-life balance difficult to achieve, which is a problem, especially in American culture. Working hard is considered an admirable quality in American workers, often to the point where workers can experience illness from stress and lack of breaks. Family leave is disappearing, and many employees feel pressured to not take any of their vacation time. Many workers do not have any paid sick leave and cannot take off from work when they fall ill, either.

It does not have to be this way, though. You may not be able to control every aspect of your job or career, but you can start making small changes here and there to ease the burden, especially if you're looking to head in the direction of freedom via self-employment. Make your workplace as hygge as possible to reduce stress and displeasure.

Adjust your attitude about work. Work is not life. You work to live; you should not live to work. Work is not the sole priority, so set limits on how much you work and when work can contact you. This mindset is not always possible in some fields. If you are on call, try to make the best of your free time to do hobbies or be with your family. Conserve your time as best you can in your line of work.

Not everyone can do what they love, but if you can, then do it without fear or doubt. Maybe it is finally time that you open your dream restaurant or quit your job to try traveling the world and make money blogging. Sometimes you may need to sacrifice money for happiness. Adjust your attitude to value happiness over money, and take a pay cut to do what you love if possible. When you die, the amount of money you made will not matter to you — how happy you were will.

Evaluate your budget to determine what you can relinquish and how much money you can safely lose if you need to change your career. Take some vacation time when you can afford it. Consider reducing your hours, or even explore new job options in a field that you enjoy. It is more important to have a life you enjoy than many expensive material possessions. Hygge encourages you to value moments and experiences over meaningless possessions and money. Just make sure you are able to make ends meet where necessary (such as rent, electricity, and groceries) and proceed from there.

Some people, such as artists, are lucky enough to do what they love. The only problem is that it is easy for these people to forget about other important elements of life as they become addicted to their jobs. If you are such a person, remember that there is more to life than your job. As exciting as your job is, you need to do other things you love, including spending time with your family or exercising outside. Never devote everything you have to your job, because your job is only a fraction of what your life is about.

MAKE YOUR WORKPLACE
SURROUNDINGS MORE HYGGE

By now, you know very well that the décor and colors used in a room can greatly affect the mood and productivity of a person. **Danish** offices look different than those in other countries because the Danish understand the work environment can influence how you work and how you feel about the work.

Whether you are working at a desk, in an office, or at home, make sure your workspace is clean and uncluttered. Being organized can stop the day from being too hectic and can make you feel better all around. Imagine how much time you will save if you are not busy looking for things in a huge mess. And think of how much better you will feel if you walk into a clear space where you can breathe and not worry about stepping on something or having something fall on you.

If you have any choice in the décor and color around you, choose light colors or white with a pattern. This ideal décor is not distracting and will not negatively affect mood or performance. You don't need tons of pictures or distracting knick-knacks on your walls or desk. However, you can really enhance your mood at work by having a few things that bring you joy, such as a nice note from a boss or customer, or a cute photo of your kids.

Some people benefit from a vision board, where they attach pictures of their goals and cherished ideals. You can use a vision board to help you visualize your goals and feel inspired to achieve those goals. Use it as a means for productivity and mood enhancement, but don't get bogged down feeling negatively toward yourself if it takes you some time to achieve your goals.

Use a comforting scent. If you have a stressful job, try a lavender diffuser to bring relaxation into your atmosphere. If you need energy, try scents like citrus or rosemary. If you need comfort in an emotionally challenging job, find a scent that reminds you of good times, and use an essential oil or scented candle to bring into your workspace. For just a few bucks, you can get a wax warmer that will diffuse scent throughout your workspace.

Comfort is key. You can't expect to work well if your environment is unpleasant and uncomfortable. Ergonomic keypads, mice, chairs, and desks can add so much comfort to your workplace. You can also use a cushion or neck pillow to make your chair more comfortable. If you can't decorate your workspace as you please, then just add little things, like a colorful tissue box or a jar of candy. Be sure to wear comfortable shoes and clothes. Even in a formal setting, you don't have to wear business clothes that make you want to faint. If you walk during your commute to work, you can wear comfortable shoes such as tennis shoes or sandals and just carry your work shoes in your bag to change into at the office. Make sure your clothes match the current weather, so that you can maintain good body temperature. Don't wear anything so tight that it digs into your skin as you work. If you have to wear a uniform, make sure it fits and loosen it by undoing a button or taking off your belt or tie during your downtime.

ATTITUDE

The way you perceive situations can greatly change how you feel about them, and sometimes it can even change the outcome. Hygge at work is all about your attitude and the way you carry yourself.

First of all, remove the urgency. Even if you have an urgent deadline, or if you are in the business of saving lives, you can reduce stress by removing the idea that your job is life or death. Your job very well may be life or death, but don't focus on that. Instead, focus on the tasks at hand. Don't think, "I have to do this by midnight, or it is over for me!" Think, "I have 'this many' steps to complete before I reach my deadline at midnight. So, this is how I will divvy up the tasks over the remaining hours." Approach things from a problem-solving angle. Don't focus on what might happen if you fail, or what you stand to lose. This attitude reduces your stress and makes work more pleasurable. When your mind wanders, use mindfulness to bring it back into focus.

Confidence is also key to reducing your stress and improving your mood. You don't feel that great when you are busy criticizing yourself or feeling inadequate, do you? Believe in yourself. Let yourself take calculated risks that will grow your business or your team's performance. Try innovative things. If you fail, learn from that experience instead of beating yourself up over it. When you are confident in your abilities, you can look beyond yourself and seek out others who are good at what they do.

Another excellent method of improving your attitude at work is to work on your cooperation skills. Cooperation is what makes businesses run well. When you are confident, you aren't egotistical and jealous of others. Rather, you are open to appreciating and working with others. You put away your ego and become open to others. That's a great way to be at work! Work will be easier when you strive to work with others and make valuable connections, without letting jealousy and ego get in the way. Your confidence will also make you more attractive to others, so they will want to talk to you and work with you.

Connect with your co-workers and have fun with them. **Work hard to collaborate with others. If you prefer to work alone, at least make water cooler chitchat to connect with others in your workplace. The day will go by faster, and you will rest easier knowing that you have co-workers who will help you out when you need it.**

Finally, keep the attitude that your work is only one part of your life. Place value on other things, like hobbies and family.

WORK-LIFE BALANCE

Hygge encourages you to live your life moment by moment. It encourages you to be with your family and friends. That can be difficult when you are stuck at work all the time, but you must strike a balance between work and the rest of your life. Devote some time to work, but use good time management to get everything done. Then set boundaries and don't work when you don't have to. Take some time for yourself and your loved ones where work may not intrude.

Work-life balance requires you to find time for things other than work. This means that you should not feel guilty or afraid of taking a vacation. It also means that you don't answer work emails when you are at home with your family, and when you are out to dinner, you don't answer work-related phone calls unless absolutely necessary. Have automatic vacation responses set up on your email that inform people when you will get back to them. As tempting as it is to respond right then and there, get back to them when you say you will, not during your time off. Most people are accepting and understanding when you set these boundaries. Without these boundaries, your workaholic nature will become the standard that people expect from you.

If your job does not allow you to have an adequate work-life balance, then consider switching jobs or even careers. It may take some time to move into a new position, but you should work for it. You need a job that does not treat you like a machine.

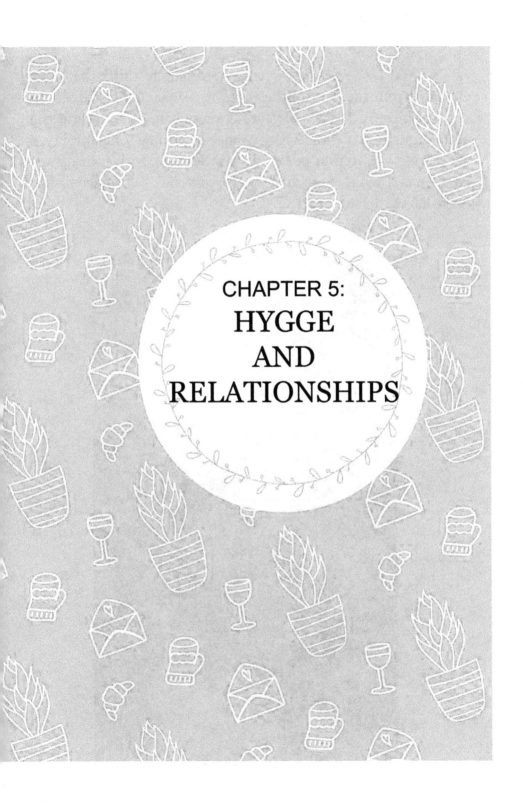

CHAPTER 5:
HYGGE
AND
RELATIONSHIPS

Wouldn't it be nice if stress and drama could be removed from your relationships? It may seem impossible to think that simply changing your lifestyle a little could make you happier in all your relationships. People spend years in therapy to try and get it right, and sometimes still fail. Hygge cannot guarantee compatibility, but it can help you to find peace in your dealings with your spouses, parents, colleagues, and children, if everyone can compromise and make a few adjustments.

FINANCIAL SECURITY

How many fights have you had involving money? Danish marriages, excluding the royal family perhaps, are much different from many other marriages around the world.

Firstly, the average age of both men and women getting married is above 30. This later age means that many individuals are already financially settled before they bring another person into the mix. No matter what age you are when you get married, strive to be financially sound before you make that commitment. If you are already married, then take some time to focus on outlining and achieving your financial goals. You should work hard together to remove any financial strife that causes problems in your marriage.

Many Danish people also do not have the kind of lavish weddings that so many other women feel pressured to host. Many Western women often seek to outdo every other woman with their weddings, and a high price tag often means years of credit card debt. Yet this competitive approach may not be the best way to start out a new family, even if the wedding is a beautiful moment. The wedding should be about the couple, not pleasing and impressing everyone else. A simpler wedding is sometimes better. Consider minimizing stress and focusing on enjoying your partner instead of having an enormous, fancy wedding.

Throughout marriage, sound decisions are made by many Danish couples to ensure savings and living only within their means. Eliminating fights over bills can bring you and your partner much closer together. Create a budget together and stick to it. If you don't need something or can't afford it, then don't buy it. Focus on enjoying the little moments together than squandering money on what you don't really need.

NO DRAMA

Drama has become a part of American culture, and everyone seems to find a way to create it or place themselves inside of it, whether intentionally or not. Then they wonder why divorce rates are so high and why they are so unhappy. Drama has no place in a healthy relationship, so picking your battles is critical. Being right isn't always going to feel good when it means going to bed alone.

Of course you will fight, but try to fight fair. Don't reduce it to name-calling and dredging up past wrongs. Fight with a purpose, and do not go to bed angry. Try to reach a resolution rather than hurting each other. You have heard it a million times, but fighting fair really is key, and that applies for all relationships, not just romantic ones.

CREATING ROMANTIC MOMENTS

In a romantic relationship, you want to create memorable moments. These romantic moments don't entail expensive dinners at fancy five-star restaurants or island vacations that break the bank. They don't involve presents of diamonds or hundred-dollar rose bouquets. Sure, those ideas are romantic, and you can practice them with your partner whenever you are able, but you can create romance even when you are broke or tired after work. All you have to do is be thoughtful and think of what your partner may want.

Offer your partner a foot rub or a bubble bath after a long day at work. Surprise them with their favorite dinner. Suggest an evening walk. Pick some flowers and present your partner with a handmade bouquet. Or try the Danish practice of taking long walks together out in nature. These little actions show that you care. When you make an effort, your partner will notice and reciprocate, and your relationship will grow stronger and better.

Also, strive for more frequent deep conversations with your partner. Conversation bonds you and your partner. It helps you get to know each other. Your partner will feel more loved and appreciated if you take some time to talk to him or her. Simply taking the time to ask about his or her day and thanking your partner for being in your life can make a world of difference. Some married couples careening toward divorce have been able to save their marriages merely by saying thank you more often and asking each other about their days.

HYGGE AND FRIENDSHIPS

Of course, your relationships are not limited to romantic involvement. You most likely have several friends and acquaintances. Your relationship with your romantic partner is not the same as your relationship with your friends, of course, but you can still practice hygge throughout your friendships. There are many different ways to keep hygge in your heart when interacting with your friends. Here are a few tips you can keep in mind to maintain hygge in your friendships:

- Take time while getting to know a new person. **When you meet someone new, you may be tempted to jump right into being close with him or her— or, on the other hand, you may not think you'd be compatible as friends. Either way, don't let your first impressions cloud your relationships with new people. Work slowly through the first stages of any relationship. This pace can make it easier for you to connect with others and to find ways to bond with them, and it can also help you determine those people whom you may not want to get to know more closely, too.**

- Set aside time to spend with your friends each week. **Lives can get busy even when you are trying your best to practice hygge, and it may not always be possible to meet up with your friends in person every week. However, make sure you're at least connecting with them weekly to see what's going on in their lives. You may have to achieve this contact through texting or phone calls, especially if your friends don't live close enough for you to drop by their houses. These types of conversations can be just as enriching when you devote your full attention to your friends and make them a part of your regular hygge routine.**

- Go out of your way to remember a few details about your friends. **You don't have to remember everything they tell you—and they don't have to do that for you, either. But if you go out of your way** to try to remember a few specifics, your friends will be happy and you'll have the joy and comfort of knowing you contributed to their happiness, too. This concept goes beyond just remembering their birthdays, and it also includes keeping track of details, like their favorite color or something they may collect. Keeping this knowledge handy can also make it easier for you to choose gifts for your friends when necessary, too!

- Spend time in person with your friends whenever possible. Of course, it's not always possible for your schedule to work out with your friends' calendars, and it may not be easy to spend time together in-person frequently. Try to reach out and offer to do things with your friends in person when you can. If your friends reach out to you, try not to turn them down every time, or they may stop asking after a while. Keeping up with a friendship can be challenging, but it can also be very rewarding. Making time for your friends is a very hygge concept and can help you feel more comfortable and happier, too.

- Don't be afraid to invite friends along for big family outings. Yes, your friends may have their own families, but they may also want to join yours for some experiences and events, too. If you and your friend both have families, why not try inviting them all along for a big group get-together? Try having a cookout in the backyard with both families involved. This way, you can spend time with all of the people who matter the most in your life, and your friend can do the same thing. You can practice hygge in this way by setting aside time to spend with people who bring you joy and comfort.

- If you fight with your friend, try to remain calm when working it out. Everyone fights sometimes; that's human nature. However, when you are trying to keep things hygge in your life, it's important to work through disagreements and problems as quickly and easily as possible. You do not have to apologize for everything when a fight happens, because fights are a two-way street. Be sure you apologize genuinely for the parts of the fight that you may have contributed to. Stay calm when you do this and don't say things to guilt or aggravate your friend further. It can be hard to learn how to recover from a fight while keeping things hygge, but it is possible to do so.

- When giving gifts to your friends, keep them simple and comfortable to stick with the hygge theme. Don't give your friends anything that is too expensive for you to fit into your budget, and don't give them presents that are too large for their homes, or that might disturb their hygge decor. Try to choose presents that are meaningful, functional, or both when gift-giving the hygge way. You may also want to try making homemade presents, which can help you incorporate your hygge hobbies into your friendships too.

Whether you are just getting to know a new friend or you're interacting with someone you've known most of your life, you can keep these ideas in mind when spending time with your friends. Hygge doesn't have to stop with your romantic relationships. Best of all, if you practice hygge in your friendships, you may be able to convince your friends to join in the hygge experience, too! In this way, you'll be spreading the spirit of coziness and comfort to everyone you know.

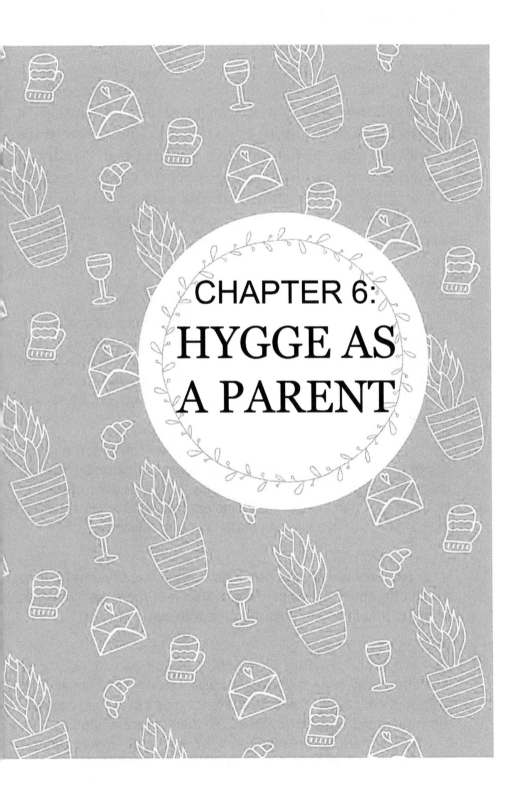

CHAPTER 6:
HYGGE AS A PARENT

The parent-child relationship is often overlooked when it comes to improving the way you feel with other people, but it is one of the most important relationships you will ever have. Your relationship with your children sets up a model for their future relationships. It is important to cultivate love, trust, and independence. Hygge can be a huge help in achieving this proactive parenting goal. Plus, trying some Danish parenting tips may give you relief if you are struggling with how things are going with your children currently. Here are some hygge tips on parenting that might help transform a chaotic home into a more loving and comfortable one:

- Redirecting represents the first line of discipline instead of going straight to spanking or time outs to modify the child's behavior, especially later in life. Many acts of misbehavior resonate from emotions that a child just does not know how to express yet. Redirect the child on how to express themselves properly, and the behavior will change. Ask them, "What are you feeling right now? Is there another way you can show what you are feeling instead of [insert bad behavior]?"

- Playing is growing. There is a reason the Montessori method is popular in schools: Play is considered an essential part of learning and development for children. Play with them often and let them use their imagination. This approach will foster excellent critical and creative thinking skills in young adulthood.

- Have children help with chores as soon as they are physically able. Not only will chores get done quicker, meaning more time for fun together, but children will also feel more self-worth in knowing that they can help an adult with something.

- Have uninterrupted time together where everyone enjoys doing things as a family. Turn off electronics and be with your kids wholeheartedly. Have meaningful conversations with them and get to know them as individuals, as challenging as it may be to consider them anything but your babies. Let them express themselves. Make sure there is something in it for everyone. Ensure that no one is excluded, and all of you are in the moment with each other.

HYGGE FAMILY MOMENTS

It is easy to create family moments that you can cherish for years to come. Even the smallest activities can become wonderful memories. From fishing trips to day excursions to local museums, use the resources available to create little moments together. You don't have to spend a lot of money to enjoy family moments.

Most people today have busy schedules, and they hardly have time to sit down and eat. Make a conscious effort to get all family members at the dinner table every evening. Talk about each other's days. This unity will create a bond with your family, making you closer as a unit. If you have a family member who absolutely cannot eat with you because of work or school, coordinate your schedules and set aside a few hours to spend time together. Just trying to spend time together will mean a lot to your family and encourage them to make time for you.

If you're looking for a hygge-appropriate family vacation, try going on a camping trip together. This suggestion may seem a little old-fashioned, and depending on how attached your kids are to their phones and electronics, it may take some work to get them to agree to go. A well-planned family camping trip can go a long way toward improving your whole household's hygge experience, as well as helping you bond with your kids and partner.

A camping trip doesn't have to be a long one to make a positive impact. Even if you just take a weekend getaway trip to the local campsite, you and your family can have a great time with each other. Don't worry about spending a ton of money on expensive camping gear or renting a cabin or RV for the trip. Just take a tent and the essentials along, and plan to cook everything you eat on-site, too.

This way, you won't be spending so much that you feel stressed by the costs, and you won't have your comfortable family experience interrupted by worries about money.

It may be a little difficult to be physically comfortable when camping, but that doesn't mean you can't be emotionally cozy the whole time. Bring along battery-powered lights and set up a cozy atmosphere after the sun goes down. If anyone in your family plays an instrument, encourage them to take it along and have a group sing-along together. Keep coziness in mind at all times when you're camping together with your loved ones and you will likely have a beautiful hygge experience that will provide memories to last a lifetime.

If you don't live anywhere close to nature, you could consider planning a staycation in your city instead. Stay in an affordable hotel or even try a hostel. Visit local museums and other nearby attractions that are affordable and easy to get to.

CHAPTER 7:
HYGGE IN THE SEASON AND HOLIDAYS

WINTER HOLIDAYS

Christmas, Hanukkah, and Kwanzaa are some of the most hygge holidays because they are naturally cozy. Invite the winter holidays into your home by preparing ahead of time. Focus more on having family gatherings with hot cocoa, singing carols, sharing stories, and making cookies together, rather than on buying the most expensive presents for each other and decorating your house more lavishly than your neighbors' homes. And don't forget that Danish Christmas tradition of giving special treats to the animals in your life, too! Remember what these holidays are about: love, cheer, family, and coziness.

Winter holiday decorations can help you keep the hygge spirit going all winter long. Don't choose noisy, bright, flashing decorations or multicolored lights. Instead, pick more muted colors and gentle themes like snowflakes, silver and gold colors, and winter forests. Choose one or two colors for your lights instead of all sorts of different colors at once. And don't decorate with items that play loud sounds or music.

Another important concept to keep in mind when practicing hygge during the winter holidays is to let your family or friends be involved with your plans whenever possible. Are you going shopping for gifts for your kids? Bring along a friend! Are you going to a friend's holiday party? Ask if it's okay to bring your romantic partner along, too. There are many ways to make sure you're spending time with the people you love during the holiday season. This togetherness can help you keep things hygge during this cozy time of the year.

You may want to invite your kids to help you decorate during the holidays, too. This collaboration can be a fun way to create family bonding experiences that will encourage your children to remain positive and upbeat during the season, too. After you decorate together, take time to settle down with some hot cocoa and a kid-friendly holiday movie.

Remember, too, that it's easy to get bogged down with the stress of the holidays. During this time of year, you're likely to encounter chaos everywhere you turn, whether it's in the form of a noisy ad or a busy shopping center. There are plenty of opportunities to get overwhelmed, frustrated, and upset when this time of year approaches, but remember that this is not good hygge. It's always essential to set aside time for yourself so you can remain calm during the holidays. This act of self-care can help you clear your mind and remain mindful enough to form lasting memories.

Remember, as with anything, hygge is not about overindulgence or stress. If you're going to be cooking often during the winter holidays, cook only what you need and try not to be wasteful. When serving your family for the holidays, don't spend a fortune on expensive ingredients when more affordable ones will work just as well—or even better. The same holds true of giving gifts during the holiday season.

Maybe you have some traveling to do during the winter to visit your family in other parts of the country. Depending on where you live, this may be a daunting task. You might have to fly or drive a very long way to get there. Although it's always important to see your friends and family when you can, especially around the holidays, try not to stress too much about this type of travel if possible. Do everything you can ahead of time to make the trip as easy as you can.

If you're going to be traveling by air, start planning far enough in advance that you aren't scrambling at the last minute and buying expensive plane tickets just a few days before your trip. Do your research and determine what you'll be allowed to bring on the plane and what you may need to check or leave behind. If you're traveling with kids or pets, learn those rules and regulations too.

If you'll be driving for a long distance, plan your route as well as some backup routes ahead of time. If you need to stay overnight on your drive to visit family, reserve your hotel rooms far enough in advance that you won't have to pay last-minute prices for them. This precaution can help you reduce the stress levels you may experience during your trip as well.

THANKSGIVING

Thanksgiving is another very important family-oriented holiday that can help you improve your hygge experience. Plan to have a big meal with your family, but remember that there's no need to overdo it. Just because a large turkey with several side dishes and desserts may be what you see on TV versions of the holiday doesn't mean you have to stress yourself out cooking so much for your family. Make enough food that everyone can get full and enjoy themselves, but tone it down whenever possible, too.

This is another holiday you can celebrate while getting your kids involved. Invite your children to learn a little bit about cooking by helping out in the kitchen. Even if your kids are very little, they can stir or decorate food (as long as you don't mind having to clean up afterward!). This way, the whole family can bond together over cooking a meal. You may even want to try putting together a meal that is full of hygge ingredients, which you can find in our section on hygge cooking later on in this book.

Thanksgiving, like Christmas, is a holiday that is about togetherness. There's nothing more hygge than spending time with the people you love and being mindful of that time so you can truly enjoy it and remember it later on. Be sure to remain mindful in everything you do throughout the Thanksgiving holiday.

Keep in mind, too, that traditions can be a nice way to practice hygge, but they aren't required. Maybe you have a tradition of making Thanksgiving dessert with your child, but now your child has gone away to college. Instead of being caught up in the negative feelings surrounding this change and allowing them to impact your hygge experience in a bad way, try to consider the way your relationship has bloomed and grown. The good feelings associated with those memories were not about making the dessert, but about spending time with your child. For this reason, you can approach this in a hygge way and make new memories by being positive and mindful of the time you spend with your child, even if you don't bake together anymore.

Don't forget to decorate for Thanksgiving with hygge in mind. This is a holiday that focuses on warm, soft colors, so use those comfortable shades of brown, tan, and yellow whenever possible in your dinner decor. Light candles and keep the lights low during your Thanksgiving dinner for a great hygge experience, too.

NEW YEAR'S

Even the New Year can be hygge with a little practice. New Year's Eve is typically a celebration that's all about making noise and partying hard. Even if you want to let loose, drink, and be merry, there's no reason you can't keep hygge in your heart at the same time. Spend this holiday with your friends and family, and don't forget to take this time to express gratitude to them for being a part of your life. When you count down to the start of the new year, practice being mindful of the experience and truly living it. Don't look at your phone or computer through the whole event!

You can also make hygge your New Year's resolution. If you're not practicing hygge yet, or if you feel like you could do better with it, make it your resolution and set hygge goals for yourself throughout the year. Just remember not to stress yourself out in learning to practice hygge. This is a process, so don't worry if you aren't getting it right immediately. Any New Year's resolution is meant to be worked on throughout the year, rather than changed abruptly.

BIRTHDAYS

What about celebrating birthdays? Can they be hygge as well? Absolutely! If you are an adult, your birthday may seem like a negative experience. You may find yourself wishing you weren't getting older, but remember that time doesn't stop for anyone, and aging is a normal and acceptable part of your life. Try not to let yourself feel too stressed out about getting older; instead, be mindful and live in the moment whenever possible. We are not promised even one more day, so be thankful and appreciative that you've been given another year to work on improving your life and experiences.

If you have children, they may be a lot more excited about their birthdays than you are about yours. Don't let your negativity about your own birthday interfere with your children's happiness about theirs—and try to integrate some of that happiness into your own birthday experiences, too. When you have kids, it's important to set aside a special time to celebrate their birthdays. Make this time all about your children and help them understand that it's a time to be happy and excited, more than just getting presents.

Sometimes, it's not possible to celebrate a birthday on the actual date. Adults usually understand this, but kids may have trouble with this concept. If this delay happens within your family, make sure you set aside time to celebrate the birthday in question even if it can't be on the right date. This approach can help your child (or even you) feel a little more special.

Decorate for birthdays in a hygge way. You don't need to go all out with an expensive cake, and you can even try baking your own cake with the help of your family for a more hygge experience.

Finally, no matter who in your life is having a birthday, be sure you give gifts that are thoughtful and meaningful in some way, or functional. If possible, try to do all three! Of course, most kids want to get toys and electronics for their birthdays, and you can give these kinds of presents too as long as you don't overdo it. Remember not to give items that are going to cost so much you end up stressing about money instead of enjoying your loved one's special day. Don't offer presents that are just going to become clutter and make life disorganized for the person you're gifting.

OTHER HOLIDAYS

While the winter holidays are possibly the most hygge, you can make every holiday hygge by really getting into the spirit. Go all out with candy for trick- or-treaters and have fun on Halloween, give your kids candy on Easter, and go to local events and spend time with family and friends for any holiday at any time of the year. These suggestions entail embracing the holidays and enjoying the moment, which signify hygge in a nutshell.

Some people feel disgruntled or annoyed when the holidays roll around. Why not enjoy yourself? The holidays don't have to be stressful or commercial, just because the media and others around you make them so. Rather, the holidays are an excuse to take a break from work, enjoy yourself, and enjoy good food. Forget about your diet. Forget about being the best. Let go of work concerns. Just allow the holiday spirit overtake you and make it a special time for yourself and your loved ones!

SPRING

Spring is a fun time when the earth begins to wake up from winter. The cold lingers, but the days are pleasant. Take advantage of the energy of spring by doing some spring cleaning and airing out your house. Go outside and show your kids the magic of nature by pointing out bird nests and budding flowers.

Although this time of the year is excellent to enjoy nature with your family, it's also still a little cool outside. It's still a good time of the year to curl up with a hot cup of tea under a soft blanket, especially in the evenings! Another nice way to practice hygge during the springtime is to sip your morning cup of coffee slowly while you admire the sunrise. You might have to get up a little earlier than usual to do so, but it can help you start your day off with a comfortable frame of mind that can keep you calm and organized throughout the rest of the day.

Spring is always a viable time to do a little spring cleaning and reorganizing, too. If you're looking for a way to improve your hygge at home, try setting aside a few days for you and your whole family to get involved with cleaning. Organize your closets and get rid of anything you may not have worn or used over the past year. Spring cleaning is not a requirement for hygge, but it is a great way to bring many of the aspects of hygge into your home during this refreshing time of the year.

Don't forget to stop and think about the way nature is changing around you as spring dawns. This time of year represents birth, fresh starts, and life. Bringing these concepts into your daily routine can help you feel more at peace and mindful of the world around you.

SUMMER

Summer is a fun time when you can enjoy yourself outside. Make the most of summer by getting in touch with nature. Plan a lot of outdoor excursions and hikes. Plant a garden and grow some of your own fruits and vegetables. If you have kids, they will love the experience of growing food, too. Take advantage of the precious summer months and the fact that school is out to spend time with your family. Embrace the short time that summer allows for outdoor barbecues, firecrackers, and sports like volleyball, swimming, or softball.

If you live in a very hot climate, it may be difficult to go outside often during this time of the year. If this is the case, try to get out in the morning before the temperature climbs too high, or make plans to go out after dark or to enjoy some sunsets. Just because it's very hot outside, that doesn't mean you can't spend time enjoying nature with the people you love. It just requires you to think a little differently about the types of outdoor activities you may want to enjoy during these months.

School may be on break for your kids, but work doesn't usually stop for adults during the summertime. It can be difficult to go to work with a positive mindset when it's hot and you just want to go on vacation. Just remember to keep up with your hygge at work, and double your efforts during summer when you may need it most.

If you're taking a summer vacation with your family, don't stress too much about planning it. Try not to spend too much money or cause yourself any additional worry about finances by taking an elaborate trip. While a big, expensive cruise or a trip overseas may sound like fun, your budget might not allow it. You can have just as much fun staying closer to home and enjoying the relaxation and comforts of a hygge vacation with your family. You may even discover some local places of interest you've never heard of before!

AUTUMN

Autumn is a cooling down time, when you can enjoy the transition from summer to winter. Use this period to prepare your house for the coming winter by filling it with candles and warm blankets. Make warm soups and teas. Harvest your garden and enjoy the fruits of your labor. If you have a lot of trees in your yard, rake the leaves and proceed to play in the piles with your pet or your kids, or even your romantic partner, for some silly fun. Go for hikes in the brisk autumn air and observe the migrating birds. These activities allow you to embrace the essence of fall.

Nature isn't the only way you can enjoy fall and bring hygge into your life at the same time. This is a wonderful time of year for wearing some of your most comfortable clothing, so don't forget to bring out those light, soft sweaters and other cozy clothes that embody the hygge spirit. Most clothes and decorations at this time of the year are available in warm, earthy colors that enhance the feeling of hygge when you see them. Stick to these autumn shades whenever possible, even when choosing the candles and blankets you'll use in your home as the weather turns cooler.

When it's brisk at night but not too cold, this is an excellent time of year to go out and stargaze. The cooler air and fewer clouds make it easier to see the night sky, and it's comfortable enough to sit outside in the evening without having to worry as much about insects as you do during the summer. If you have time and are able to do so, drive away from the city lights and explore nature to stargaze with your family. You can also take this opportunity to learn and teach your children about the stars you can see from your region or even from your own backyard.

During the fall, prepare to decorate for and celebrate Halloween and Thanksgiving with your family. Have fun with this, but do so mindfully and without being overwhelmed by too many requirements you may set for yourself as the holiday season approaches

WINTER

Danish winters are cold and dark and seem to last forever. Do the Danes let the winter get them down? No, they make the best of winters by inviting warmth, coziness, and cheer into their homes. Don't allow snow and darkness to upset you; rather, make a game of playing in the snow and use winter as an excuse to make a lot of warm, delicious food. Bring out your comfy sweaters, sweatpants and slippers. While shoveling snow and salting the driveway, sing songs to keep you warm and have your kids help. It may be challenging to keep your spirits high during the coldest times of the year, but it is possible with the right hygge mindset

Winter is the best time of year to practice making some of your favorite comfort foods. If you're not used to cooking, you may want to start with something easy like chicken noodle soup or homemade bread. You can also try making brownies, cookies, and other fun treats for your family. If you're a little more experienced in the kitchen, why not branch out with recipes you've never tried before that include comforting ingredients? You might even want to make something completely unique for your next big holiday meal. Don't forget to get the kids involved, or invite your partner or friends to join you for a cooking activity.

CHAPTER 8:
FOOD AND DRINKS

Did you know that the concept of hygge comes with its own diet? Well, it's not exactly a diet. It is not guaranteed to help you lose weight. It is not even something that should be in used with every single meal. But keeping hygge in mind when you're cooking and eating can help you get the full effect of this lifestyle. With an emphasis on comfort food, great smells, and warmth, how could you not want to give it a try?

SCANDI COMFORT FOODS

If you never had Scandinavian comfort food, you are truly missing some wonderful cuisines. There is something special about every aspect of this food, and there is nothing that says hygge more than sitting down to slowly enjoy a delicious, homemade meal with friends and family. That is truly the point of this idea: to eat in comfort. There is no rush. There is a steady conversation throughout the meal that you savor, just as a meal is meant to be. Can you incorporate a meal like this once a week? If you would like to try, there are many hygge recipe books available, as the concept is gaining popularity around the world and in many cultures. In a hygge cookbook, you might find comfort food recipes involving ingredients such as:

- Duck
- Potatoes
- Rye Bread
- Quinoa Salad
- Apples

WARM DRINKS

Hygge drinks are traditionally meant for those cold winter nights spent curled up in front of a fire. The aromas are soothing, making you think of your childhood, the holidays, and pure warmth, and so is the temperature of the drink itself. It shouldn't be hard to think of something warm you like to drink, but just in case, here are some of the best hygge suggestions:

- Apple Cider

- Coffee

- Herbal or Green Tea

- Hot Chocolate

A HYGGE RECIPE FOR EVERY MEAL

If you have never cooked any Scandinavian comfort food before, or anything even close, you might be wondering what to try. **Baking is a huge part of the Scandinavian cuisine, but you can't live exclusively on bread and cookies, as much as you might like to. So, we have prepared a suggestion for each meal to get you started. In sum, we offer three days of choices to try a new comforting meal with your whole family. The best part is that many of the recipes for hygge meals can be prepared together as a family, allowing you to spend even more time with your loved ones. This time together is a precious commodity, if work and school always seem to get in the way of quality time.**

For breakfast, try an apple turnover or similar pastry. **Many Europeans have their sweet treats in the morning to get a boost for the day. This tradition has been working for them for many years. Why not try your hand at it and see how you feel?**

For lunch, nothing says "hygge" better than a warm and hearty soup. **There are many varieties to choose from that are all delicious. However, pumpkin soup is by far the general favorite. You can dress it up any way you want and drink it right from a large mug.**

For dinner, why not try something savory? **Roasted pork is a common staple at the Danish dinner table. Pair it with a baked potato for an indulgent meal that does not involve anything fried or pre-made. This is the exact kind of meal you can savor at the table with your loved ones.**

There are many places you can find hygge recipes online. Here are three sites to get you started with hygge cooking:

- http://www.organicauthority.com/discovering-danish-food-with-9-recipes-to-make-you-feel-the-hygge/

- http://www.self.com/gallery/13-healthy-hygge-foods-for-the-coziest-day- ever

- https://www.brit.co/hygge-foods-recipes/

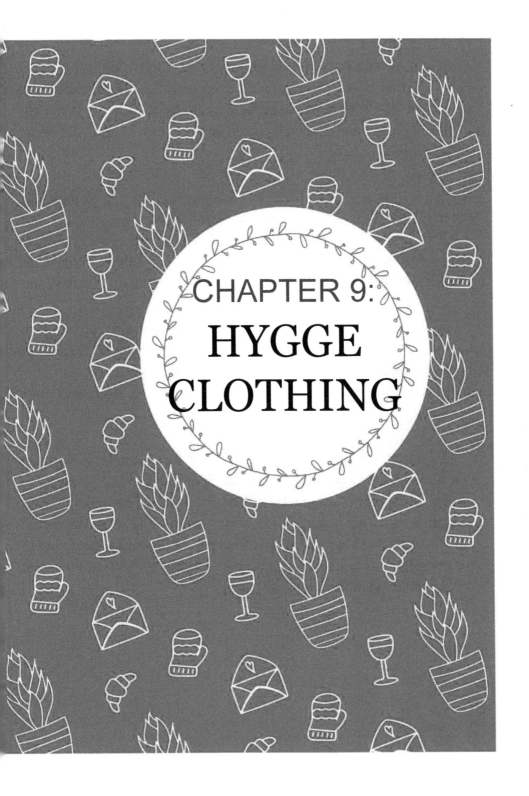

CHAPTER 9:
HYGGE CLOTHING

Hygge does not place strong emphasis on external appearances. Rather, it focuses on how you feel. It is better to be lounging on the couch in sweats enjoying yourself than looking like a beauty king or queen. While looking fashionable has its benefits, it is not the most important goal in the hygge lifestyle. You will enjoy life more if you relax.

Danish clothes are often simple and functional. They don't look bad, but they don't sacrifice quality for appearance. Wearing simple, clean, quality clothes is essential to your comfort. Clothes with pockets are useful for carrying things. You want to select clothes that don't restrict your body or make you hold a ridiculous posture all day long.

Go for a good fit, not a tight fit. Also, go for materials that feel good to you. Cotton is light and breathable during summer. Warm wool and wool blends are nice during winter. You can get the most out of sweat-wicking polyester when you are engaged in strenuous tasks or sports.

Shoes should also be comfortable. Why wear skyscraper heels when you have to walk, or tight shoes that hurt your toes and give you blisters? Instead, wear practical shoes that fit you well. Sometimes you must sacrifice beauty for comfort—otherwise, your day could often be disrupted by your aching feet. An oozing blister is not worth the compliments you'll receive. It's better to buy shoes that fit so that you are able to walk around with ease.

HYGGE SPRING CLOTHES

Spring clothes are some of the most comfortable out there. These clothes are often made of soft fabrics that allow your skin to breathe while still keeping you warm enough on cooler spring nights. They are usually available in pastels as well as soft, muted earth tones, which are all excellent color choices for a hygge wardrobe. Don't forget to bring a jacket along when you go outside during the spring, especially in the earlier part of the year. Pick clothes that give you lots of room to move around comfortably while remaining warm enough for this season.

HYGGE SUMMER CLOTHES

Stay comfortable when it's hot outside by focusing your hygge on lightweight, breathable, cool clothing. Choose shorts or shorter skirts so you can enjoy the feeling of the fresh air and breeze when you spend time outdoors. Pick tank tops and t-shirts, and bring along a light jacket or sweater for cooler nights. At this time of year, it can be fun to dress in bold, vibrant colors, so be sure you pick colors that make you feel comfortable, and happy when you look at them. As always, choose items for the comfort they can provide, instead of the current fashion trends

Many people may feel pressured to wear fashionable swimsuits at this time of year. Remember hygge even when choosing your bathing suit! Pick something you feel comfortable in—physically as well as emotionally. Don't force yourself to wear something you wouldn't normally choose just because it may be what's in style this year.

HYGGE FALL CLOTHES

In the fall, look for clothes that feature warm hygge-friendly colors like brown, gray, and cream. You may still choose thinner fabrics at this time of the year, but you'll want to dress in layers so you can add or remove clothing as needed depending on the weather. You may also need to have a raincoat handy at this time of the year, so pick one that's comfortable to wear and doesn't make you feel overheated or weighed down too much when you have it on. Even though you may be tempted to wear stylish autumn boots, it's better to pick clothes for comfort, so keep this in mind when choosing your shoes at this time of year, too.

HYGGE WINTER CLOTHES

This is the time of year when your clothes can really incorporate the hygge lifestyle. Choose clothing items that make you feel warm and cozy inside and out. Go with soft, plush fabrics and be sure to wear a coat that's lined for extra comfort. Try wearing stockings or very thick socks with your outfits to keep your feet and legs warm and toasty when it's very cold outside. And don't neglect your hands and face! Wear gloves and a scarf and hat. For best results, try knitting or crocheting these items yourself, or wearing ones made by someone you love if you aren't able to make them.

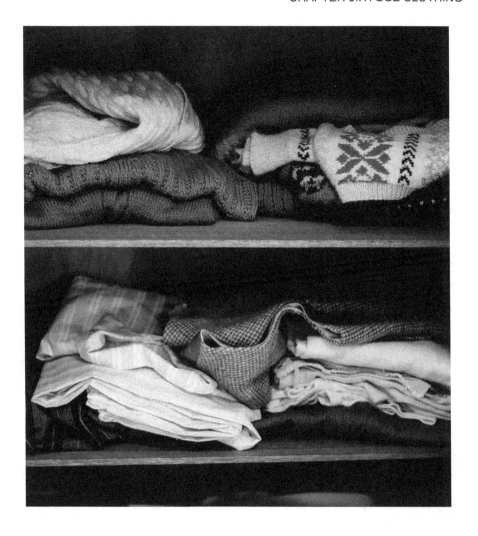

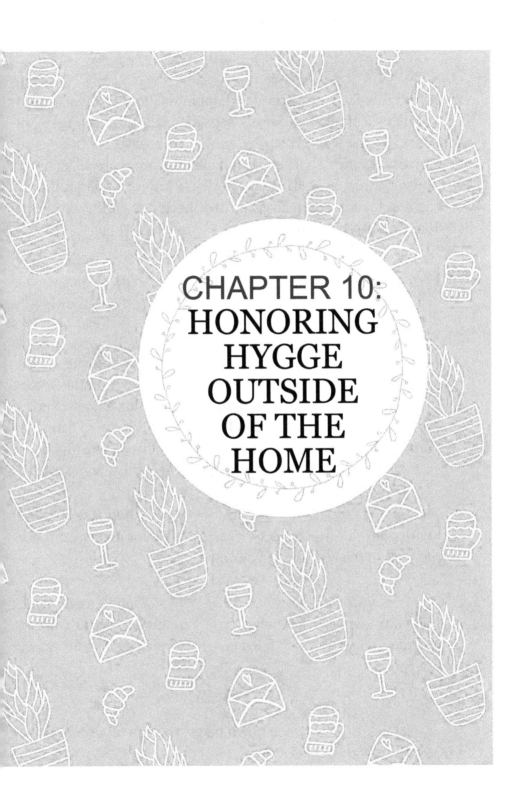

CHAPTER 10: HONORING HYGGE OUTSIDE OF THE HOME

Deciding to live the hygge lifestyle doesn't mean making your home your only place of comfort and staying there all the time. You can experience this Danish method of happiness anywhere you go. In fact, Danish vacations and family activities fall right into many of the principles you learned earlier in the book: ease, coziness, and togetherness. Picnics, short trips, and playing games are all a part of the Danish culture, as well. Peruse the list below for some additional ideas on how to incorporate hygge in all aspects of your life, including activities outside the home.

15 IDEAS FOR HYGGE ACTIVITIES

1. Cook a special meal together as a family. While this suggestion may seem like something you would only do within the home, you can actually make this happen on vacation as well. Rent a hotel room or a condo with a kitchen included, or go camping and cook your meal together over an open fire. There are many ways to cook with your family whether you're at home or not.

2. Play a board game or do a puzzle together. Just like cooking with your family, this activity is portable for any vacation or for fun in the comfort of your own home

3. Have a picnic in a quiet and serene place. Plan this excursion on your own or with people you care about. If you go on a picnic alone, be sure to tell someone where you'll be for safety purposes.

4. Take a family bike ride through the country or on a nearby beautiful trail. If you don't own bikes, you can often rent them for the day from bike stores.

5.   Take a road trip and stop at one spot chosen by each family member. This may take some planning ahead of time. Ask the people in your family where they'd like to stop, and don't tease or laugh at the places they pick, even if some of them are not stops you would choose to make on your own. This practice will ensure everyone feels included equally.

6.   Take a weekend camping trip. If you can't get away long enough for a longer camping vacation with your family, why not take a short camping trip over a weekend? You may also want to wait for a long weekend from school or work to plan this trip.

7.   Travel somewhere where it snows and play in the snow together. Depending on where you live, it may be hard to find a place where it snows without having to travel by plane. If it's going to take extensive effort to take your family to a snowy place, this may be better suited as a winter vacation than a quick trip.

8.   Enjoy hot chocolate by a fire and watch a family movie. Make this experience even more exciting by offering a hot chocolate toppings bar and letting everyone decorate their cocoa the way they want to. Plan to do this often and take turns choosing the movie so everyone is actively involved.

9.   Go fishing together. Do you know how to fish? You might not, but even if you don't, you can learn along with your kids. There's no reason why this activity can't be a fun family experience, even if you don't know how to do it yourself. Be sure to check local laws and regulations before you head out.

10.   Read a classic book as a family. You can either do this aloud or plan to read separately and then discuss the book together

at a later time. Make this more hygge by going to the park and sitting in a quiet location while you all read together on the weekends. You may also be able to do this experience in the evenings after school while it's light enough outside.

11. Bake a dessert together. Just like cooking together, this can happen inside or outside the home. If you bake together inside the home, you may want to share your dessert with people in your community or with friends.

12. Go caroling together. If you're looking for a way to bring more hygge into your holidays, why not try caroling as a family? Be sure to practice this safely and do not go into strangers' homes while caroling.

13. Locate an open space and play a sport together. Whether it's the park, a community baseball field, a gym, or a beach volleyball net, try getting active and playing sports with your kids. They don't have to be formal games, and you can just play around together while spending time with each other.

14. If you have a dog, take it for a long walk and take note of all the animals, insects and plants you see. This is a great way to incorporate hygge with caring for your pets. You may also choose this time to teach your kids more about proper dog care, too.

15. Go on a short hike to a waterfall. If you live somewhere near hiking trails or walking paths, try taking one or more of these on weekends. Whether you're on your own, with friends, or with your whole family, hiking to a waterfall can give you a sense of peace and mindfulness while allowing you to experience nature's beauty.

HYGGE HOBBIES

A hygge hobby is anything that offers you stress relief and comfort. You should engage in hobbies that bring you into the present and allow you to forget your worries and stress. The more engaging and absorbing a hobby is, the more mindful it will make you!

Try some of the following hobbies to improve your hygge experience overall:

- Yoga. This practice can help you become more mindful and therefore more hygge.

- Jogging. By working on your health and getting outdoors more, you'll be enjoying hygge even more.

- Knitting, embroidering, and other crafts. Being creative as a hobby is a fun way to encourage your own self-expression. It can also be something fun you do in your personal space inside your home.

- Painting. This creative activity can be fun to do outdoors or inside.

- Hiking. Take an easy hike if you're not experienced, or go for a more strenuous one if you want to challenge yourself while still having a chance to get outside.

Anything you enjoy that can increase mindfulness is a good hobby to incorporate into your hygge lifestyle!

HYGGE AND TRAVEL

The Danish love to travel, and for good reason! Taking in the world around you and appreciating the experiences travel brings you is essential to being happy. If your budget allows, try to travel as much as you can. Although we've already talked a little about traveling at the holidays, this section can give you more in-depth tips about hygge travel plans.

Many Americans associate travel with stress. To be truly hygge about travel, you want to take it slow and enjoy your time abroad or wherever you may be visiting. Don't plan every moment, but instead allow experiences to happen as they will. Not everything needs to be perfect, and often plans fall apart, so don't expect to strictly follow a schedule. Instead, wake up each morning, decide what you want to do, and do it. Tailor experiences to your preferences.

With that said, you may feel stressed if you go into a vacation with zero plans. Make sure you at least plan for how you will get around your vacation destination and how you'll get back home when you're finished traveling. It's also a good idea to plan your hotel or other lodging ahead of time to reduce stress. After that, being spontaneous is much more relaxing.

You should also maximize your comfort. Bring a neck pillow on planes or long car rides, as well as a soft, plush blanket. When traveling by air, you'll be much more comfortable with noise-cancelling earplugs or headphones while on the plane. If traveling with children, bring plenty of comfort items for them as well. You should also plan to bring distractions for them, since they may get more restless than adults during long trips.

Many people fail to plan for a cold draft on planes or buses, so be sure to bring warm socks and a comfortable sweatshirt. Sleep when you can. You may consider bringing your own pillow and blanket to help you sleep in unfamiliar rooms. Bring the items you need to feel at home, such as hand sanitizer, a spray that smells like home, or headphones to listen to music that soothes you. While it is great to try new foods, you should also bring comfort foods that remind you of home in case your stomach doesn't agree with the foreign foods. Don't forget to bring any medications you might need for the duration of your trip so you aren't scrambling to find them in a strange place.

Be sure to stay within budget. There is nothing quite like financial insecurity to ruin the pleasure of travel. It's acceptable to stay at a budget hostel or motel instead of breaking the bank for a five-star hotel when you'll be out and about for most of the day anyway. Taking the train or bus can be cheaper and less stressful than driving. There is no need to splurge on first class when coach is perfectly functional. Find ways to save money and shop deals on sites like Travelzoo, Sherman's Travels or Scott's Cheap Flights.

Picking beautiful destinations is key. You want to enjoy traveling and enjoy the world around you. Experiencing new things and beautiful places will help you feel hygge immensely. Even if you can't afford to go overseas or far away from home, you can have many amazing experiences when you travel. Most people don't even realize how many unique sights there are near their own homes. With "staycations" becoming more and more popular for Americans, finding hidden gems near your hometown can be a great way to vacation without spending a lot of money. Why not look for "off the beaten path" locations near you? Find a few walking trails or other nature spots close by and stay in a cheap hotel room or campsite for a short but sweet getaway if you are unable to afford a bigger vacation.

No matter whether you plan to travel far away or stay close to home, the important hygge concept to keep in mind is expanding your horizons as well as your family's. Make new experiences for yourself and your family when you travel. Find out about cultures you may not know much about, and practice new languages. Discover the history of a location—even if it's your own town or region. And in all things, remain mindful, cozy, comfortable, and hygge. Taking a trip will help you feel peaceful and joyful in no time.

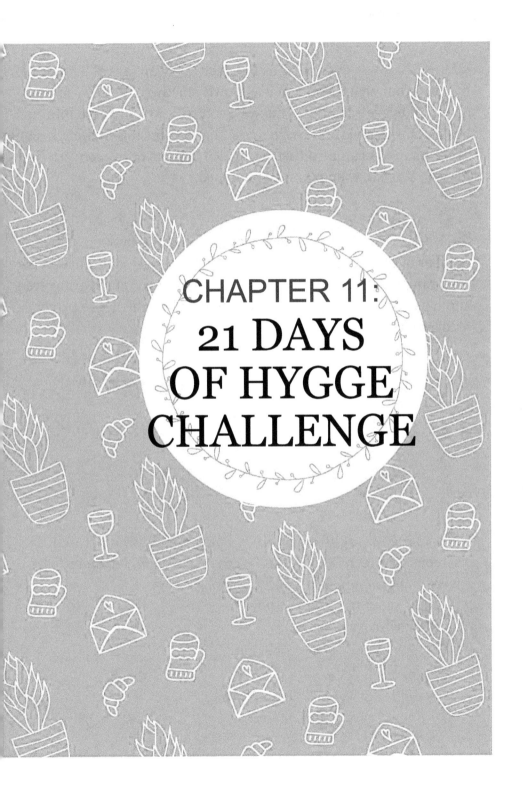

CHAPTER 11:
21 DAYS
OF HYGGE
CHALLENGE

Now that you have read up on the hygge lifestyle, we want to leave you with a challenge. This is a challenge to try 21 days of living with hygge in your heart. Think of it as slowly starting a diet. Try one new aspect of hygge each day. This way, you will not only ease into this new happy lifestyle and begin to see the changes it is making inside of you, but you can also find out which aspects of hygge work best for you. You can then plan to go forward.

So, it's time to go get a calendar and choose to try at least one thing each day. You could do this however you want—by increasing the number of things you do each day as the weeks go on, or just trying one brand new practice each of the 21 days. Get your family involved and have fun with it! You'll already be fulfilling the hygge principle of togetherness.

21 WAYS TO INCORPORATE HYGGE INTO YOUR DAILY LIFE

Day One:

Set aside a night without screens and tech. Spend time with your friends and family talking, playing games, and bonding with each other.

Day Two:

Bake bread from scratch. If you have kids, let them help, too!

Day Three:

Bring something from outdoors inside (rocks, flowers, nature décor). Just be sure it's something safe to bring inside.

Day Five:

Find a quiet, comfortable place and read a book in your at-home personal space.

Day Seven:

Have breakfast in bed. Make it the night before, so you can grab it and return to bed to enjoy it.

Day Nine:

Start a gratitude journal. Don't forget to pick a journal with a cover that brings you joy.

Day Four:

Have a movie night with friends and family. Refer back to Day One and turn off your electronics during the movie for best results.

Day Six:

Have a relaxing stay-in-your-pajamas day. If you have to work and can't make time for a whole day, try spending your free time after work in your pajamas instead.

Day Eight:

Take a stroll through a park or nature preserve. If you don't live near either of these, take a walk outdoors anywhere.

Day Ten:

Use candlelight instead of electricity for a night. Play music as a family or read a book together during this time.

Day Eleven:

Watch the sun rise or set, preferably with a loved one.

Day Fifteen:

Try beginner yoga. You can use videos from the internet and save money on an actual class at a studio!

Day Fourteen:

Give yourself an at-home spa day with natural scrubs and soaps. Pick soothing, rejuvenating essential oils.

Day Seventeen:

Listen to calming music. If you do so while meditating, that's even better!

Day Thirteen:

Have a hot chocolate night with the family. Have fun add-ins like marshmallows and sprinkles so everyone can make their cocoa special.

Day Twelve:

Have a warm drink at a quiet café with an old friend. Or, if you need some time to yourself to unwind, do this activity on your own instead. Be sure to bring a book so you're not glued to your electronics!

Day Sixteen:

Hug everyone you care about freely. Just be sure to give them a fair warning and don't startle them!

Day Nineteen:

Hold hands with your spouse or other loved one while watching a movie. Sit close to each other and enjoy each other's company.

Day Eighteen:

Take a walk around the neighborhood in sweatpants and a comfortable shirt. Take time to feel the breeze and make note of the smells and sounds around you.

Day Twenty-One:

Color in an adult coloring book. Better yet, make it a family experience and have every one color together!

Day Twenty:

Lay in bed and talk to someone, either on the phone or in person.

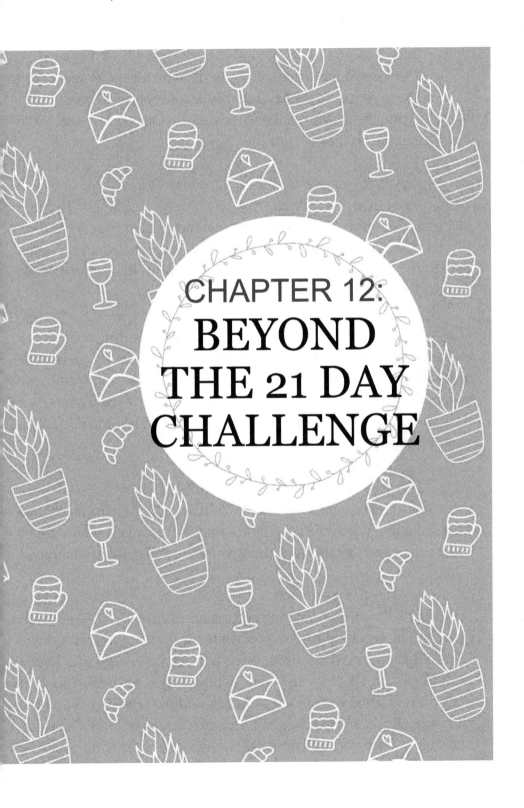

CHAPTER 12:
BEYOND THE 21 DAY CHALLENGE

Hygge does not just stop after you check off the activities on the above list. Once you practice the hygge lifestyle for three weeks, you won't want to return to your typical hectic and routine! You can take hygge beyond the 21 days challenge in the previous chapter and make it a permanent fixture of your life.

Remember that hygge is about living in the moment, so forcing it and worrying about how to achieve it is counterproductive. Instead, just make an effort to enjoy at least one moment of your day. Soon, this lifestyle will become such an ingrained habit that you won't even have to think about it. You will want to do it naturally, so it won't take any work on your part.

Make an effort to take care of yourself. Take a few minutes to relax at least once a day. You owe it to yourself to be more hygge in your attitude and your routine. Not every moment will be comfortable or enjoyable; you can't always forget about your worries and cares. But if you practice hygge mindfulness at least once a day, you will find a new enjoyment of life.

Also, make your home and workplace a hygge atmosphere. These measures will help you enjoy a more fulfilling life. When you change your décor and wardrobe to be more comfortable, you will have fewer distractions and irritations plaguing your day and ruining your mood

Try starting a new pleasant morning routine to set the mood for the present day. Don't watch upsetting news stories on TV or scroll through glamorous posts on social media that fill you with envy. Don't hit the ground running, already burning energy in a hectic dash to get out the door in time. Instead, enjoy yourself. Wake up early and do some yoga or sip some tea without a feeling of anxiety and panic. Enjoy a leisurely breakfast with your loved ones. Get ready and enjoy the physical sensations of showering, getting dressed, doing your hair, and applying makeup. Try to take in the sunrise and the birdsong of early morning.

Getting your friends and family on board can help you make your life more hygge as well. You can all enjoy the precious moments together while omitting distractions like phones and TV.

CONCLUSION: EXTENDING YOUR HAPPINESS

As the title of the book, "The Danish Secrets of Happiness: How to Be Happy and Healthy in Your Daily Life," suggests, all this information is aimed at helping you find happiness in our currently chaotic world. It can be challenging to figure out what brings you true happiness, but this book is intended to provide you with the groundwork you need to get started. Happiness is something many of us, even in privileged societies, find ourselves chasing. However, the chase may be exactly what is making us unhappy. With hygge, you can slow down and find happiness and peace in the simple pleasures, which is a feeling that cannot be bought. Living the Danish way can be a rewarding experience for the whole family, so remember to be grateful and cozy and spend time together!

A SWEDISH GUIDE
LIVING
LAGOM
TO A BALANCED LIFE

MAYA THORESEN

REVIEWS

Reviews and feeck goes a long way to improve this book and the author as well .If you enjoy this book, we would greatly appreciate it if you were able to take a few moments to share your opinion and post a review on Amazon. I need to know your opinion so that I can find areas where I can improve. Reviews help me, and then I can help you more!

https://mailchi.mp/752b5b4dd620/mayathoresen

Living Lagom

A Swedish Guide
to a Balanced Life

MAYA THORESEN

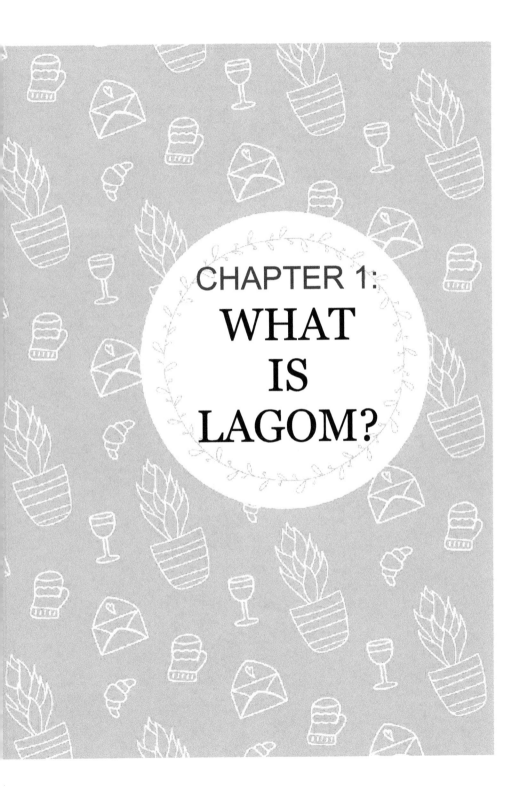

CHAPTER 1:
WHAT IS LAGOM?

Lagom (pronounced [la:g:Jm]) is a Swedish word used to describe the perfect state when something is neither too much, nor too little, it is just enough to make you satisfied. It can be used when talking about anything from the weather Know the amount of milk you pour in your coffee. If the question starts with "how much?" the typical answer in Sweden is "lagom." There are a few words that can be used to relate to lagom; for example, "enough," "moderate," and "balanced." Each of these concepts contributes to the overall meaning of lagom. The true meaning of lagom, however, is a way of expressing when something is just enough.

Etymologically, the term "lagom" is a combination of the two words "lag" and "om." Centuries ago, there was a lack of food, resulting in only one plate of food per household, which had to be enough to go around the table. No one at the table could take too much food. In Swedish "lag" means "team," or "table," and "om" means "around." "Lagom", therefore, implies around the table. This explanation makes sense, although nowadays, historians and etymologists believe that this may be a myth constructed more recently.

Lagom is used to describe a feeling of satisfaction or when something is enough. We all have a different perception of when we are content and satisfied, which makes the definition a bit difficult to pin down, but this is the essence of lagom. There is no general description or measurement of how much lagom is, which makes it quite a complicated concept. There are as many definitions for lagom as there are Swedish people. How much each one considers to be satisfying is a matter of taste, and it can be difficult even for the Swedish to understand what someone else considers to be lagom. Of course, it is a constant source of discussion and friendly debate amongst friends, families, and couples when one of them wants lagom and gets either too much or too little. This usually happens when one person neglects to ask the other how much he or she considers to be lagom. It is easy to give someone else what we ourselves believe to be the right amount. Of course, frequent misunderstandings are expected, especially when new acquaintances are still determining each other's definition and taste. However, the misunderstandings are neither serious nor the source of any huge conflict at all amongst the Swedish people, as they are considered a part of everyday life. For most individuals, there lies a silent agreement to disagree on the definition and accept that everyone thinks differently.

If there is no real definition of lagom, then why use it? To those who are not Swedish, the definition is strange and complicated, and it can be debated whether anything is truly lagom. Distinguishing lagom is like comparing food that is too hot or not hot enough, too sweet or not sweet enough, and so on. Despite these constant complaints, the Swedish people are quite content with everything when asked to seriously consider the situation. Perhaps these minor complaints are a way for the Swedish people to connect to each other and start a conversation. They might be onto by something; accepting things as never quite lagom is being lagom in itself. From this aspect, the concept is not about a useless word, but instead is about a useful and satisfying concept that makes the Swedish people happy.

The question still remains: Why is lagom something to strive for if we are not able to agree on what lagom is?

It is complicated to apply logic and reason when lagom cannot have a proper, quantifiable definition. There is one more aspect of lagom, which we have not talked about yet. If we dropped the point of defining lagom, then the whole point is that there is no definition. Perhaps the meaning of lagom is to figure out what it is for you and live accordingly without being so concerned with other people's thinking.

Let's examine this further. In Sweden, the general mentality is "each to his own"In other words, don't interfere in other people's lives when they have not asked for it, and let them express their opinions and live life on their terms. Lagom is something that needs to be figured out independently and then applied to life. There is no right or wrong definition of lagom; it is a grey zone that is defined independently and expressed differently by each person. The aspect of lagom and its definition is beautiful because it holds space for interpretation for each person.

Lagom cannot be defined as one single, universal statement, but an independent one that each individual has to define on their own. As your life and your perspective changes, so can your definition of lagom. Lagom is always in tune with you.

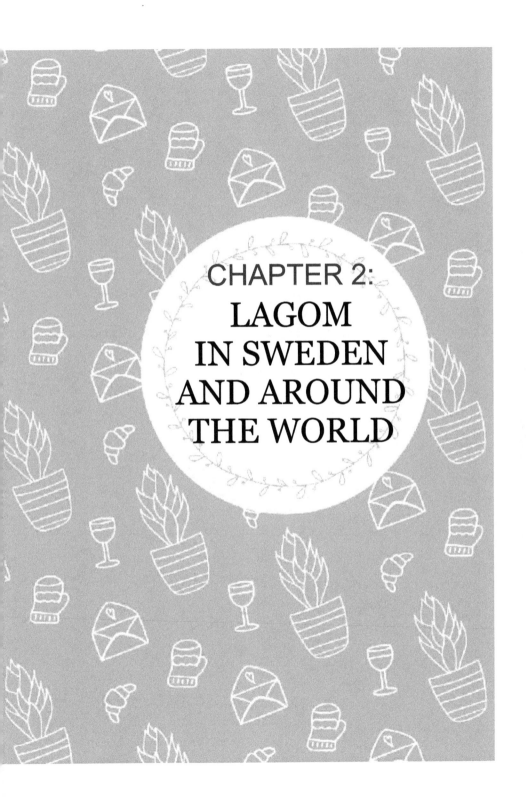

CHAPTER 2:
LAGOM IN SWEDEN AND AROUND THE WORLD

In this chapter, you'll learn how the Swedish people view lagom, which is different from how the rest of the world may see it.

The Swedish have a somewhat complicated relationship with the word lagom and all that it stands for. The lagom lifestyle is a way of thinking and acting that is deeply internalized in the Swedish way of being, and they don't tend to consciously think about it. It is a life that goes on and on in a nice little track of decisions, and the fact that it does so makes lagom go by unnoticed, perhaps even ignored. Alternately, other Swedies are sick and tired being labeled as lagom. They feel stuck in a rut and tend to feel ashamed at being considered moderate, seizing every opportunity trying to break free. It is not easy to explain why some Swedes have this feeling. Perhaps they don't want to be labeled and and wish to escape from the term, while others just ignore or live with the label that has been imposed on them.

Besides the anti-lagom population, Swedish people in general are more careful to keep their lives lagom-style, rather than living too large or putting themselves in a situation where they are noticed. The Swedish can be regarded as content being labeled "lagom" as they live their lagom lives. Perhaps some of them have become more comfortable with being lagom as the rest of the world picks up this lifestyle.

In the previous chapter, you learned about struggles with defining the term "lagom." This difficulty comes from other countries being more and more fascinated with the phenomenon and adopting it for their own. It is interesting how a rather small country like Sweden can influence others to live a different kind of life in order to maintain balance. Some Swedish state that they maintain the lagom lifestyle because they find it as the easiest way to live a sustainable, healthy, happy, and balanced life. Some of them consider lagom to be the perfect interstitial path in a divided world full of contradictions and non-consequent advice. Lagom allows you to enjoy all the little pleasures in life and still be healthy and satisfied.

To the rest of the world, lagom seems to be a clever way to make a difference and turn certain events around in order to make things better. In a world where we face huge environmental issues and are constantly searching for ways to save the planet, lagom might, in fact create a more sustainable lifestyle. For example, instead of buying food that goes uneaten, people can buy only the necessary amount. This goes for clothes and everything else as well; buy only what you need and what you will use. To the rest of the world, lagom might be a way to describe the "quality over quantity" mindset. This can save you time and money in the long run. This is also applicable to the "work as well as home" balance many of us struggle to find. Instead of working too much and spending little time with our children, strive to do everything lagom-style to make time for both the business and pleasure aspects of ife without facing a burnout. These are some of the reasons why the world is fascinated and inspired by Sweden and lagom.

While some of the Swedish people are sick and tired of being caught in this grey scale of life where everything is lagom, in moderation, and just enough to satisfy them, people in other parts of the world are turning their eyes to Sweden as a leading example of a sustainable, healthy, and happy lifestyle.

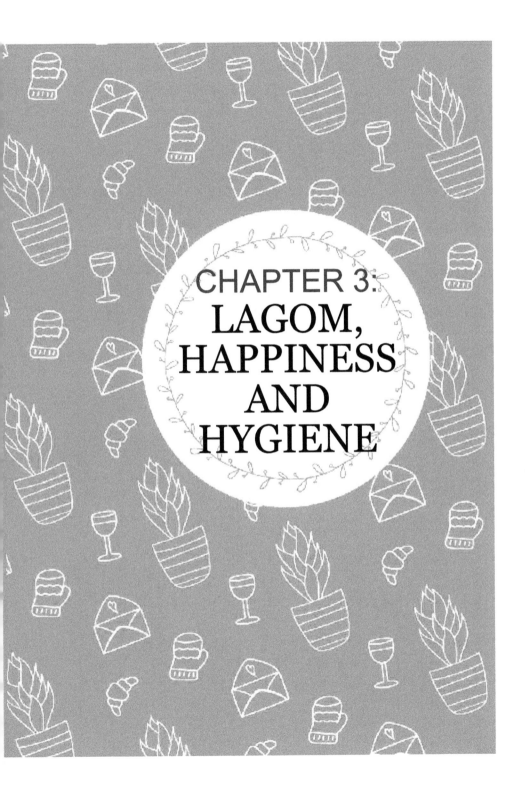

CHAPTER 3:
LAGOM, HAPPINESS AND HYGIENE

We have already touched on how lagom can be connected to happiness and how it can lead to a more harmonious life. In this chapter, we will dig deeper to discover more about this idea. In this book, when we raise the subject of lagom and its connection to happiness, keep in mind that we don't talk about happiness about an event or situation, but instead, we are referring to a subtle and calm feeling of joy. This type of feeling does overwhelm you if you aren't used to it, but rises from a place of satisfaction. You might also think of it as contentment.

Although some groups of the Swedish population are trying to break free from being labeled "lagom," Sweden has paved the way for a new method of achieving balance and also more happiness. Settling for lagom when you could be striving for more is not a bad idea; in fact, the Swedes are on to something. By settling for lagom, they don't take on more responsibilities than they are able to, and in doing so, they apply a sense of self-preservation and self-care. When settling occurs in your job and your life, there is no urgency to strive for more for yourself or for your family. Use the time to do things you enjoy that create happiness. Working constantly is not healthy for you, your mind, or your family, as your energy is depleted by work. Applying moderation in your life will create happiness and can increase the amount of contentment already present in your life.

To accomplish lagom, take a look at your life and analyze what is important to you. Take a look at your habits and consider how you can improve them. What's better way to use some extra time than to create a lifestyle that makes you happy? What makes us happy is specific to the individual, but whatever you like to do, using lagom in your life will make some time for your favorite things. It is important to remember that time is not the only connection between lagom and happiness -- it is contentment. Considering things to be "just good enough" rather than striving for perfection can save plenty of irritations and help you to a stress-free life. This process can take time, though. The first efforts of transitioning into a lagom mindset can be frustrating, as things can begin to pile up and not be completed. It is like quitting smoking or caffeine. It is frustrating at first, and you might have to abstain from certain things, but after a while, happiness will come easier to you than before.

When talking about lagom and finding happiness, there is another phenomenon worth mentioning. In Denmark, they have a concept called hygge [pronounced hoo-ga]. Hygge can be described as a warm, cozy, and comfortable atmosphere where you take the time to enjoy the good things in life with the people you love. Hygge is an activity, or a state of being, whereas lagom is a view on life and a way of living. Despite the differences, there is a connection to be found between hygge and lagom. They are both derived from a longing for slowing down and keeping things simple. Lagom is all about balance and moderation, and when experiencing hygge, you are spending your time in a moderate way. It is an easy-going atmosphere where nothing is too much or too little, but just lagom. Therefore, hygge is a lagom state of being, despite the lack of connection overall. While lagom and hygge are different connections to living and feeling, they are similar in cause and consequence. Apply lagom to your life to achieve balance and to find more time for the things you love to do. This extra time saved can be spent with family, friends, other loved ones, and hobbies in a cozy atmosphere called hygge. It all works out as a circle of being cozy and happy in your home as energy and money should not be wasted to enjoy life. In other words, hygge is lagom completely.

Like lagom, what makes something "hygge" is a matter of taste. To some people, it might be meeting some friends over dinner, catching up after work in a nice coffee shop, or a movie night with your family. The point of hygge is to be calm and cozy- to pass the time in such a way that you will be energized instead of burning negative energy constantly. Filling up your positive energy like this will result in a balanced, happy, and content life. Furthermore, enjoying the little things in life can improve your ability to handle stress like a mediocre job, a mean colleague at work, or any of the small, annoying things that occur in everyday life. Lagom and hygge are very similar concepts, although they also have some differences. It's important to understand both of these concepts separately when you're trying to live a lagom lifestyle so you can more easily determine which elements to incorporate into your way of living. Read through the lists below to help you get a better idea of what to expect from both hygge and lagom. This way, you'll know when you're practicing a habit that falls into one more than the other, and you'll be better able to choose the right methods of improving your lifestyle regardless of which category they may fall into.

ELEMENTS OF HYGGE:

- Hygge is designed to help you feel cozy. At its core, this concept is all about comfort and coziness in every aspect of your life. The warmer, the better!

- Hygge could include curling up and being comfortable in your favorite clothes, with your favorite blanket, and surrounded by soft lighting while you enjoy a hobby that helps you relax.

- Hygge focuses a lot on textures and relies on soft fabrics to help create the sense of coziness required for living this lifestyle.

- Colors associated with hygge include neutral and earthy tones such as cream, beige, tan, gray, dark brown, gold, and silver.

- There's more to hygge than just physical comfort; it is also about being comfortable around your friends and family. This concept involves relaxation and the kind of happiness you feel when you're with the people you love.

ELEMENTS OF LAGOM:

- Lagom is about enjoying the quality of your life instead of feeling like you have to increase the quantity of the things you own. minimalism is where lagom really shines. The more minimalitic you are, the better you'll be at bringing this concept into your hone and life.

- One of the key points of lagom is making sure you live as sustainably as possible to reduce your carbon footprint. Your relationship with the environment is crucial to ensuring you have a great lagon experience.

- Textures aren't important in lagom, but it is a good idea to introduce curves and gentle, flowing lines into your interior spaces rather than sticking with sharp, hard lines throughout your home to inspire an organic sense of peace of mind.

- When possible, choose handcrafted items as well as foods that are made from healthy, organic ingredients for your lagom lifestyle.

- Colors associated with lagom include neutral tones such as tan, off-white, and soft gray, as well as slot of starkly constrating tones found in minimalist decor, such as black and white.

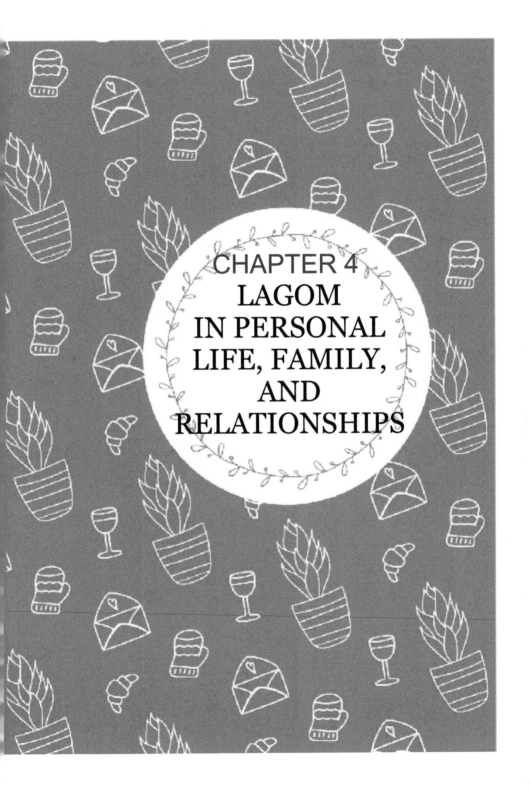

CHAPTER 4
LAGOM IN PERSONAL LIFE, FAMILY, AND RELATIONSHIPS

Now let's talk about how to apply lagom to your personal life, your time with family, friends, and others. Plus, you will learn how to set aside time and energy to enjoy special interests and hobbies.

We are encouraged from a young age to be social; spending time with others and working well in a group is a characteristic that is rewarded in today's society. Communication has always been stressed in society; in fact, guidelines for good people skills can be found in the New Testament. In Peter 4:8-9, we can find the following: "Above all, maintain constant love for one another, for love covers a multitude of sins. Be hospitable to one another without complaining". Social skills have been important for ages, but they are even Far more important today in both business and personal life. With the influence of technology, online marketing, and social media , it is even more important to stay social in order to be noticed and successful in your career. During spare time, staying connected to social media may seem relaxing but psychologically it isn't ideal for resting, as it keeps the mind alert. For some reason, being introverted and enjoying time alone and offline is almost considered an undesirable trait, and there are even courses to teach us how to overcome this behavior and become more social. It is a challenge to stay balanced and disconnect once in a while when the world is encouraging us to be online and connected constantly.

The Swedish, however, have a reputation of being somewhat cold and distant to strangers and to each other despite the want and need for social skills in their society. The truth is that the Swedish are not really anti-social. Most of them are just as social as everyone else, but they inherited the mindset of leaving each to his own. This concept, combined with their lagom lifestyle, gives them an air of solitude-seeking and loneliness in their life. The Swedish behavior is actually quite healthy and something for the rest of us to adopt. In Western society, we are forced to be social at work, in school, and wherever we spend our time during the day. Sometimes, the expectations are extremely high; we are expected to spend time with family, talk to coworkers and clients, study with classmates or teachers, and be cordial with colleagues and peers. This is stressful and can be exhausting. In the evening and on days off, it is still expected from others and society to be social when all our bodies need is sleep and rest. Filling up days with things to do leads to exhaustion and lost interest in passions. When transitioning to the lagom lifestyle, you might get frustrated and even hate doing things you usually enjoy with others just because you have been forced into everything and forced away from yourself. Therefore, it is important to keep in touch with yourself and your own interests in order to enjoy all of these social events that are quite nice when you find the perfect balance in socialization.

In Sweden, when people sit alone on the bus, or avoid talking to each other while waiting in line at the supermarket, they are creating a balance between social commitments and encouraging some recovery time. It is true that the Swedish are keener on minding their own business than many others, and this contributes to their lagom lifestyle. They could chat with the person next to them, but they don't, because they value personal space and privacy. In these situations, lagom does not mean staying at the house, locking yourself inside, and having scheduled time alone, because that does not work either. Instead, lagom is about being quiet while riding the bus or standing in line. It is not forced downtime alone, but rather a good compromise to recharge and have more energy once you get home to your family. By applying lagom this way, the Swedish have cracked the code of balance between being social and being alone. Instead of bending over backwards trying to keep up with all the social events and commitments, the Swedish people take care of their alone time. They spend time alone, either by themselves or with their family, allowing themselves time to recover and recharge from the social pressures of the world.

Once you take the time to rearrange your busy schedule and recharge properly, it is possible that you will want to take up a hobby. Hobbies are often the first to get eliminated as we become busy with work and family, despite their numerous health benefits. As discussed earlier, applying lagom leads to an increased amount of free time that you can use to recharge. Recharging energy levels can bring love and joy to previously enjoyed hobbies. The love and joy you find in a hobby can also generate new energy that you need for work and family. Of course, a hobby can be social, but by being alone once you have the freedom to do whatever you wish to your mind can rest for a moment, and you can go deep within and follow your inner voice. Lagom is about balance, and if you are usually very social, this is a way to find balance.

On the other hand, if you are less social, and prefer spending time alone, lagom might mean that you should put yourself out there more. This could look like creating time to spend with friends, family, and others. If you are generally quiet at work, try talking to your colleagues and ask them questions to spark conversation. Meet new people outside of work by joining a group or an association to share time with others who have like-minded interests. Meeting new people can bring fulfillment in life and joy to new life experiences.

Finding a balance between work and home life can be hard to accomplish, but it is completely possible. If you find yourself working hard with no time left for pleasure, then you might want to take a look at the situations You are able to control. The solution may not always be obvious, but by thinking about your options and asking friends, family or co-workers for help, a solution will arise. If you can, try talking to your boss about having too much on your plate, say no to colleagues who want help when you are too busy for your own work, or help each other out to succeed at the same goal. If you find that you are working at a dead-end job, try to find a new job or a new career. Everything is possible to achieve balance in your life.

Sorting out your priorities can be hard. To find the lagom balance, write a list of things you feel like you have to do and write a list of things you want to enjoy doing. Then, prioritize the list, putting them in order, starting with the most important. Throughout the day, cross them off as you go. The key here is doing a little of what has to be done and a little of what you enjoy doing. At the end of the day, both lists will have things crossed off so you can see what was accomplished. This will leave you feeling satisfied and content with how the day was spent. In other words, doing more with the time you have can help you enjoy moments of lagom with family and friends.

The Swedes are not better than anyone else at saying no, and prioritizing and enjoying their relationships and hobbies. Although they do have the concept of lagom to guide them, they don't think about how to spend more time with their families and friends. Perhaps the Swedish have a natural longing for solitude, helping them to stay balanced in their social engagements.

Lagom is a lifestyle to help you achieve balance within yourself and in your life. Spending time with family and friends while still enjoying hobbies and interests alone is important to your health and mind. Instead of striving for perfection, just do what you do as well as you can. No one will thank you for overdoing it instead of settling for a little bit less.

The next important matter when it comes to living a lagom life is how to create a good balance. The right amount of balance is up to you to decide. If you love your job and don't have anyone waiting at home, then feel free to spend more time at work. If you recharge by being surrounded by people, then spend more time with others. An introvert may need more time alone to feel balanced. Think about your wants, needs and obligations, and see what can be rearranged to achieve that balance in life the lagom way. Remember, everything in moderation.

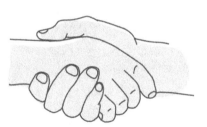

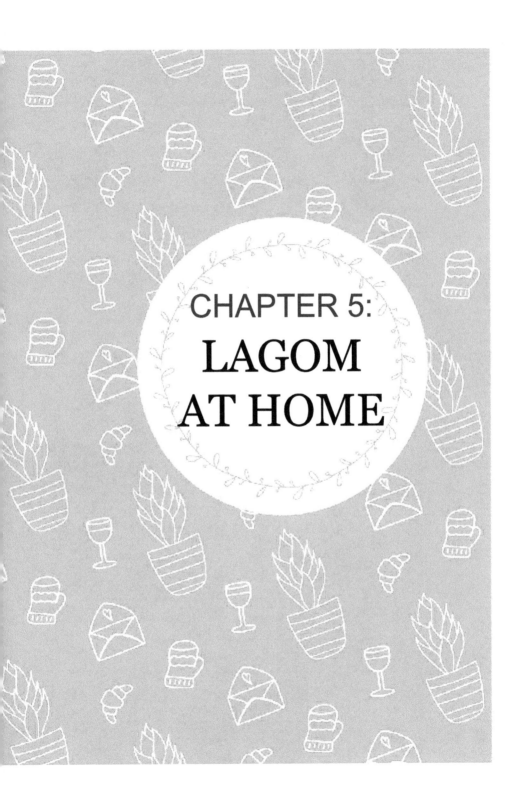

CHAPTER 5:
LAGOM
AT HOME

Lagom is not only useful for creating harmony and balance between work and life or between socializing and time alone; it is also a useful tool to make your home a peaceful, relaxing and comfortable space to dwell in. In this chapter, you will learn to focus on creating the most peaceful home you have ever had - the lagom way.

Starting with the home itself and its decorations, there are a plethora of things to make your living space a cozy and comfortable place to be. Do you have any furniture not being utilized? Start with that. Get rid of furniture that is never used, to eliminate the clutter and fill your home with items that bring you joy and happiness. Then continue on, eliminating decorations, cushions, and curtains you don't like don't use in your home.

It's important, when working on your lagom lifestyle;to understand how to decorate your home in a way that is best suited to this concept. Remember that lagom is all about living a life that is not too little and not too much. This means that you shouldn't rush out and buy all new furniture to replace every item you own, especially when some of your existing furnishings may work just fine for a lagom home. On the other hand, it does mean you might want to cut back a little and make some different design decisions that can help you bring balance to your living space.

BEDROOM

- Try painting the walls white, off-white, or gray in your bedroom to create a cool and relaxed space. If you desire color, you could paint one of the walls and/or use colorful bedding.

- Decluttering is usually the first step toward creating a lagom bedroom of any kind. Clutter is common in bedrooms, so take your time organizing and don't forget to donate or sell any items you no longer wear that may be cluttering up your closet space.

- If you have a window in your bedroom, choose a window treatment that will allow you to let in light during the day.

- Don't hang too much on the walls, and take care not to set out a lot of knick-knacks around your bedroom either.

- For your bed sheets and covers, choose simple, soft, neutral colors and stick to solids instead of patterns or prints. Don't cover the bed with unnecessary decorative pillows, and consider removing the headboard and footboard for an even more minimal look.

LIVING ROOM

- Stick to beige or gray walls in your living room for the perfect lagom mood.

- Set out houseplants for a touch of nature and greenery to freshen up your living room. Remember not to overdo it with plants, however, or the space may look too cluttered.

- Go with sheer curtains at the windows to encourage more natural lighting.

- Use smaller area rugs instead of larger carpets to break up the space visually and help things look more minimal overall.

KITCHEN AND DINING ROOM

- The wall color in your kitchen should be cool and relaxing.

- Choose a wooden dining room table if possible to bring something natural into the space.

- Don't clutter your counter space. Put away appliances you aren't using regularly, and be sure to let everything have its own visual space to sit on the counter.

- Try choosing vintage chairs and other similar repurposed furniture in your kitchen and dining room.

BATHROOM

- White bathrooms are a great place to get started with lagom. Since many bathrooms are already painted white or off-white, you often won't have to worry about changing the wall color to get started.

- Try lighting candles in the bathroom, especially if you don't have the option to use a lot of natural light in this space. Be careful, however, not to leave these candles unattended and to only use them when you're in the bathroom.

- If clutter is a problem in your bathroom or if you have a very small bathroom, consider bringing in a set of simple white shelves with cloth baskets to store your must-haves and linens for easy access.

This will help clean up the space visually without making it too difficult to find what you need in your bathroom when the time comes.

Home is a place to relax, spend time with your family and escape from your social engagements, work, and demands from people outside. Having a home that includes things you love can bring joy, confidence, and happiness to you and others around you. Having a cluttered home can be overwhelming, which can bring stress to your life instead of relaxation. Remember that you own your things, not the other way around.

ELEMENTS OF LAGOM

- Lagom is about reaching a calm and peaceful state through decluttering and organizing your home.

- Lagom can be a great stepping stone to Zen, but the two can also exist separately.

- Lagom can be used to help you reach and maintain a happy and satisfying life.

ELEMENTS OF ZEN

- Zen is an Eastern philosophy that originated in Buddhism but has come to mean, in the Western world, a calm and meditative state of being.

- Zen can be achieved through lagom; decluttering can help you become more Zen.

- You can feel more energized and less stressed by reaching Zen through lagom.

- Connecting these two can let them work together to give you a wider perspective in the world.

When it comes to material goods, it is not better to have more. In fact, owning many things only gives you more to clean, more to replace when broken or worn out, and you will probably spend more time searching for lost items . You should absolutely have what you need, but don't fill your home with nice things only to fill empty space or to show off to occasional visitors. Instead, try to adopt a "less is more" approach to your home. How much your home should contain is up to you, as it is a matter of need and taste. Feel free to have curtains, cushions, a wine glass collection and those nice,expensive dinner plates you only use for Christmas, but take a look at your life and what you really need, what you think you need, and how much of everything you need. Don't forget to only keep and buy things you truly love and care for. Even if you need an item, don't keep it if it does not make you smile. Sell the old one or give it away and invest in a piece that makes you smile instead. Remember, the definition of lagom is up to you and differs from person to person.

Many people say they need more storage space or smart solutions to store things in the already existing storage areas of their homes. What most people actually need is to clean out their spaces and sort out what to keep and what to get rid of. A home that is clutter-free is more harmonious, allowing you to come home from work feeling relaxed and comfortable. Of course, decluttering your home takes work, and it can take a long time before you are completely done, but once your home is properly organized and neat, you will find yourself at peace. There is always something to declutter, like that junk drawer in the kitchen or bedroom, or underneath the sink. Who knows, the process could become a hobby you enjoy!

Another cluttered mess that can impact the home environment and your life is your wardrobe. Getting dressed in the morning can be both a pleasure and torture. Many of us mere looking at our clothes and thinking that we have nothing to wear. Decluttering your wardrobe the lagom way can get rid of this anxiety-driven nightmare.

Begin by emptying your closet; is recommended to get a good picture of the state your current wardrobe is in. One of the best methods for decluttering your closet has been popularized by Marie Kondo, and it's a good idea to check out her suggestions and ideas if you're looking for more in-depth information. To summarize, pick up one item at the time and consider how much you like this item, how much you can identify with it and how useful it is in your everyday life. Only keep the things you use, love, and feel are right for you. It is not necessary to make it into a complete capsule wardrobe with a limited amount of pieces. The point is to keep it organized and simple so that you have a wardrobe that expresses your personality. Create a wardrobe where you can easily find the perfect combination for each occasion, where the clothes fit together nicely, and where clothes are made in materials of good quality.

After you have organized your current wardrobe and gotten rid of things you don't want, write a list of things you need to complement the rest of your wardrobe. Another great tip regarding clothes is to plan out your outfits for the week ahead, saving you time and agony in the morning. The Swedish use lagom to simplify their wardrobe and as a result, have more time for other tasks, such as making and eating a nice breakfast, instead.

We have talked about our homes and wardrobes, but how can you shop the lagom way? The Swedish love to shop, but they are conscious buyers. Being a conscious buyer means buying only what you need, considering quality over quantity and always following your taste. The perfect way to buy only what you need is by making a list. It does not matter if you are buying decorations for your home, clothes, or food; think about what you need and write a list. The Swedish love lists! Also, avoid impulse buying. If faced with a situation where you are standing in a store wanting to buy something, consider its use in your life. If you cannot come up with one, walk away. Also, think about quality over quantity so items can last longer when it comes to clothes, furniture, and decorations. This way, you buy fewer the things you will enjoy them for a longer time.

We have talked about our homes and wardrobes, but how can you shop the lagom way? The Swedish love to shop, but they are conscious buyers. Being a conscious buyer means buying only what you need, considering quality over quantity and always following your taste. The perfect way to buy only what you need is by making a list. It does not matter if you are buying decorations for your home, clothes, or food; think about what you need and write a list. The Swedish love lists! Also, avoid impulse buying. If faced with a situation where you are standing in a store wanting to buy something, consider its use in your life. If you cannot come up with one, walk away. Also, think about quality over quantity so items can last longer when it comes to clothes, furniture, and decorations. This way, you buy fewer the things you will enjoy them for a longer time.

When shopping with moderation, think twice before buying anything. It may seem dull to shop the lagom way, but it can be delightful spending time looking for one perfect, thoughtful item instead of multiple not-so-good items. This will save you time and money, and you will become happier with each buy. Before shopping, consider the following questions:

- Do I need this item?

- When will I use it? (Think of at least one specific moment in the near future when you will wear or use this item.)

- Can I afford this? (Don't consider the price tag, instead consider how many times you can wear or use this piece. An expensive thing can cost less than a budget alternative if used more frequently than the cheaper option.)

- Do I want this for myself, or is it something I want because everyone else has it? (Only buy things you want; don't buy anything because someone else says so.)

- Do I already have this or something similar at home to use instead?

- Will I be able to sell this when I no longer find it useful (Even if you are uncertain about a purchase , determine if it can be resold later on. Selling things for someone else to use saves money and incorporates sustainable living habits.)

Sometimes an impulse can meet the criterias of a good bargain. If faced with an impulse buy, after using the questions above, use this trick: take a picture of it. Go home and sleep on it. If you are still thinking about the item and can envision its functionality in your home or life, then you can buy it. Most of the time we don't crave these impulses the next day, but if we do, it may be a good item to buy.

Buying the lagom way can bring happiness, joy, and comfort to you and others around you. Less things means more space and time. More space means that your home will be easier to clean and to keep things tidy on a daily basis. Now you will have more time for other hobbies or interests because you're not spending as much time cleaning. A wardrobe that is simple and easier to choose from will leave more time and energy for the day. Fewer things means more money. Selling the things you don't want to keep and earning extra money encourages sustainability. Decluttering your home will make it appear open, neat, and clean for guests and yourself.

All of these tips will save you energy and time to allow you to do things you love with the people you love. Declutter, stay organized and find suitable solutions to keep your living space tidy to turn your home into a relaxing and calm place where you find peace and recharge.

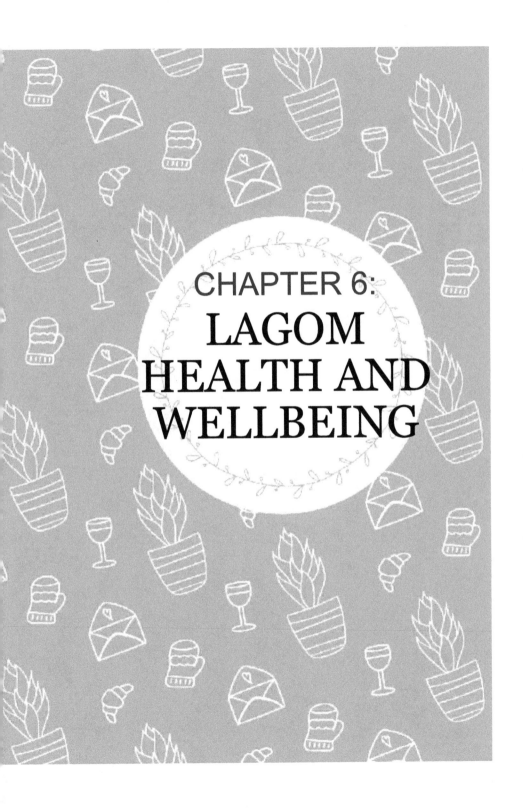

CHAPTER 6:
LAGOM HEALTH AND WELLBEING

Discussing the impact of lagom when applying it to relationships, life, and home can help decrease stress and increase time, money, and energy for things you want to enjoy. Lagom is not always about the materialistic relics in your home or how you feel in social outings; it can affect how you feel within yourself, too.

In Sweden, people like to move their bodies and exercise, not only because they need to achieve anything, but because of how it makes them feel. Swedish people might not be known for being the most competitive people when it comes to sports, but they do move frequently. They exercise every day, including taking walks and riding bikes instead of driving. They take the stairs instead of the elevator, and so on. The Swedish like to keep their bodies healthy, and in a recent poll, only 9% of Swedish people stated that they never exercise at all[1]. Marathon training, Viking races, and Iron Man races have become a trend lately for even the average Swede. Although these races are rather extreme, they have become increasingly popular. Despite the Swedish fascination for exercise and the positive impact it has on the body and mind, they are cautious not to overdo anything. Instead of exercises specially for the perfect body, they work out in order to achieve the accomplishment itself and for the feel of it.

But not all Swedes specially are interested in these extreme workouts, and even those who are dedicated to them are careful not to overexert themselves. They are careful to have lagom and balance between working out their bodies and their minds. Exercising is something that needs to fit into the work and life balance, and this can be challenging. They work to maintain a balance between activity and rest as well as between work and life, and instead of having only the toughest workouts, they go for a hike in the forest for a day or do something else that balances exercise with family life while still

---

bringing tranquility. You can definitely have a balance and still keep up with an exercise routine.

Hiking and spending quality time with your family can be considered relaxing while still being physical activity. It is relaxing because not only are you working your body, your brain is also getting a mental rest while enjoying a hygge moment with family in the forest or by the sea. This can also aid in recovery and boost energy levels.

In general, the Swedish love spending time in nature. It does not matter if they are going for a run, spending the day with their kids in the park, or spending sunny summer days by the sea;. Spending time outside can boost your body because it keeps you active the sun delivers much-needed vitamins to the skin. Most of the time we are indoors working, studying, or spending time alone or with others, and we forget how much our bodies need us to stay active.

Health and well-being are not the only benefits of physical exercise. It is also relaxing and exercises the mind. We spend our days with a lot of incoming information, and it is hard sometimes to tune out and let the mind rest for a moment. In Sweden, meditation, mindfulness, and yoga have become increasingly popular in order to balance a hectic lifestyle. Not everyone loves meditation, and certainly not all people love yoga,but many things the Swedish do, such as spending time in nature, saying no to certain events to be with family, and taking time to recover is considered mindfulness and gives life a nice touch of lagom.

Closely related to the subject of health and exercise is your diet, The Swedish try to prioritize eating solid, home-cooked meals made with clean and healthy ingredients as much as possible. They prefer spending mealtimes at the kitchen table with their families, and to most people in Sweden, good food is important to the overall well-being. They do eat junk food moderately but shy away from microwaveable dinners or anything containing chemicals. They use real butter despite the calories instead of eating light products that contain additives that are generally not good for your health. It is easy to find and buy organic food, and they are dedicated to buying locally produced food to support small businesses. Food transportation from non-local distributors can take time, and as a result,the food is not fresh once it reaches the store. Transportation also contributes to pollution which also encourage the Swedish to buy locally. They love to eat good food, but in the true sense of lagom they do not only want it to taste good, they also want it to be healthy.

Finding healthy food that is not chemically treated, organic and locally produced is easy in Sweden. You can find these foods both in the local supermarkets and in local farmers markets. For those who are inexperienced or don't have time to grocery shop, using websites like Blue Apron and Hello Fresh, can be helpful, since you can order your groceries online and have them delivered straight to your home along with healthy recipes.s. The ingredients used by these companies may not always be sourced locally, but they do come from family-run farms and are sustainably grown. There is something to fit every food choices in your life: vegan food, vegetarian, easy-to-cook food, and grocery bags with organic food if you would prefer that. The Swedish people strive to live the lagom way regarding their health. While you might find these concepts new and time-consuming, the Swedes do it quite effortlessly by incorporating several of these concepts together. For example, they relax from work by spending time outside with their families, and while doing this, they get exercise, relaxation and family time all wrapped up in one. They cook a delicious and healthy meal and eat with their family, which combines a healthy lifestyle and spending quality time with family.

In Sweden, the National Food Agency (NFA) provides guidelines on how to eat to get all of the important nutrients the body needs,there's a discussion amongst the Swedish whether they should be trusted or not since some of their advice is contradictory to certain people's beliefs regarding what is to be considered healthy food. This is not a proven fact, but in Sweden, people following specific diets, for example, Paleo and LCHF, dislike that the NFA recommends the Swedish to eat plenty of pasta, bread, and other carbs. Whether you trust these guidelines or not, they are created to help people live healthy lives by recommending a balanced diet. The NFA guidelines state to fill at least a third of your plate (preferably half of it) with vegetables and/or fruits, but the Swedish love their traditional dishes, but are not afraid to mix things up with influences from different corners of the world.

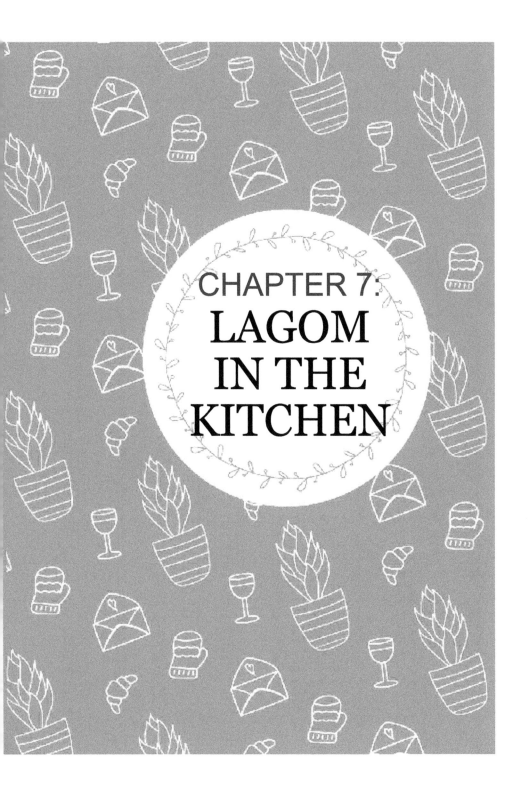

CHAPTER 7:
LAGOM IN THE KITCHEN

To encourage a healthy lagom lifestyle, here are some classical Swedish recipes to try at home. As an added bonus, we have included some non-Swedish recipes that are delicious and fit the lagom lifestyle. There are also tips on how to make your own snack food, since making things yourself is usually healthier. This way you will get a nice overall view of how lagom can be applied practically to all aspects of life.

Before we get started, it is necessary to point out these recipes have been slightly altered. We have added some veggies to classical Swedish recipes, because when these dishes first became popular, the Swedish population did not have access to many vegetables due to the cold and difficult climate. Today, fruits and vegetables are imported, and the use of greenhouses has made it so that that access to these ingredients is easier than ever before. The Swedes now eat more veggies, salads, and fruits along with their meats and starches.

BREAKFAST

Breakfast is considered the most important meal of the day, especially in Sweden. It is common to eat cereals or granola with milk or yogurt, sandwiches, and porridge. Although there has been an increasing trend in eating overnight oats or drinking a smoothie, the traditional breakfast dishes are still the most popular ones. Here we share a recipe for simple granola that you can add your favorite flavors to and modify to your taste. You also get easy-to-make oatmeal porridge that will give you enough energy to last all the way to lunch without a mid-morning blood sugar crash .

HOMEMADE GRANOLA WITH YOGURT

INGREDIENTS

- 2 cups raw oats
- ½ cup natural mixed nuts (or nuts of your choice), raw
- ¼ cup sunflower seeds
- ¼ cup flaxseed
- ¼ cup coconut flakes
- 1 tbsp honey or maple syrup
- tbsp olive oil
- Cinnamon and cardamom to taste Ingredients:
- cups raw oats
- ½ cup natural mixed nuts (or nuts of your choice), raw
- ¼ cup sunflower seeds¼ cup flaxseed
- ¼ cup coconut flakes
- 1 tbsp honey or maple syrup 1 tbsp olive oil
- Cinnamon and cardamom to taste

DIRECTIONS

1. Mix all the dry ingredients together in an ovenproof dish with olive oil.

2. Season with Cinnamon or cardamom to it and bake at 300 degrees Fahrenheit for 30-45 minutes. To ensure the granola toasts evenly, mix the granola every 10-15 minutes while baking. If you are allergic to nuts, you can add some other grains and seeds. If you don't like cinnamon or cardamom, you can use other spices of your choice. Leave to cool down before putting it in a jar. Add dried fruits such as raisins, apricots or cranberries once the granol for a fruity flavor and added nutrition.

OATMEAL PORRIDGE

INGREDIENTS

- part oatmeal
- parts water A pinch of salt

DIRECTIONS

This one is so easy it is fail-proof, and anyone can do it.

1. Take one part oatmeal and two parts water, add a pinch of salt and cook until the porridge is firm but not glue-like. If it is too loose, then cook Longer; if it is too hard or has the same texture as glue, add more water and stir.

2. Serve the porridge with fresh fruits and berries and milk, if you like. Use almond milk, coconut milk, or lactose-free milk for a dairy-free alternative.

SANDWICHES

If you're a breakfast sandwich eater, there are some healthier lagom alternatives. In fact, the sandwich is not a bad option since it is versatile and you can make anything with a sandwich! Start with sourdough bread and fill it with a wide range of healthier options like hummus or cream cheese instead of butter, and top the spread with your favorite vegetables. Or, use a cream cheese spread and add cold chicken, some green leaves such as spinach leaves,arugula, or tomato with a yogurt dressing for the perfect flavor and texture. The options are endless!

If you prefer having eggs in the morning, eat up. Eggs are an excellent source of protein and good fats. Plus, the Swedish eat a ton of eggs, boiled, fried, or poached, on a sandwich. They also eat scrambled eggs and bacon for breakfast at times. Keep lagom in mind and eat everything in moderations; there really are no other rules here.

SWEDISH BREAKFAST SANDWICH

INGREDIENTS

- 2 slices of rye bread
- ½ sliced radish Anchovies to taste 1 egg

DIRECTIONS

1. Bring a small pot of water to a boil, then add egg while the water is boiling.

2. Bring a small pot of water to a boil, then add egg while the water is boiling.

3. Boil the egg for 6 minutes or to desired doneness.

4. Let the egg cool. Peel and slice the egg.

5. Toast or broil the rye bread and top with egg, anchovies, and radish.

LUNCH AND DINNER

All of these recipes can be served as either lunch or dinner. Of course, the Swedish do eat out, but not on a regular basis. In Sweden, eating out is saved for celebrations and for an occasional indulgence, rather than as part of everyday life.

CLASSIC SWEDISH MEATBALLS

All of these recipes can be served as either lunch or dinner. Of course, the Swedish do eat out, but not on a regular basis. In Sweden, eating out is saved for celebrations and for an occasional indulgence, rather than as part of everyday life.

INGREDIENTS

- 2 tbsp olive oil
- 2 pounds ground beef, pork, or lamb 1 diced onion
- ½ cup breadcrumbs
- ¼ tsp nutmeg
- ¼ tsp allspice
- 2 eggs, separated
- Salt and pepper to taste

DIRECTIONS

1. Heat 1 tbsp olive oil over medium heat until just simmering, then add onion and cook 3 minutes, stirring occasionally. Remove onion from the skillet.

2. Combine ground meat with breadcrumbs, egg yolks, and seasonings. Mix until thoroughly combined but be careful not to over-mix.

3. Roll into about 24 meatballs.

4. Heat remaining olive oil and brown meatballs on all sides.

5. Serve the meatballs with boiled or mashed potatoes and brown sauce.

Traditional meatballs are served with pickled cucumbers and lingonberry jam with grilled tomato, a mixed salad on the side, green beans, peas or broccoli.

STEAK WITH OVEN ROASTED POTATOES AND BÉARNAISE SAUCE

Here is another classic dish in Sweden that if for summer barbecue.

INGREDIENTS

- A steak of your choice
- Béarnaise (Homemade or store bought) 1 pound small red potatoes
- 1 tbsp olive oil Salt to taste Pepper to taste
- French herbs to taste

DIRECTIONS

1. Cut the potatoes in two or four, and season with olive oil, salt, pepper, and French herbs. Roast in the oven, 225 °C for about 30 minutes.

2. Season the steak with salt and pepper. Grill or fry steak to your preferred temperature.

Serve the steak with the béarnaise sauce and roasted potatoes. Serve with in-season vegetables along with grilled (or fried) tomatoes, asparagus or green beans. Add a mixed salad on the side, grilled (or fried) corn-cob or anything else you and your family like.

HOMEMADE BÉARNAISE SAUCE

INGREDIENTS

- 2 egg yolks
- cup plus 1 tbsp butter 3 tbsp minced shallot
- tbsp red wine vinegar 1 tbsp lemon juice
- 1 tbsp chopped tarragon Salt and pepper to taste Parsley to taste

DIRECTIONS

1. Melt 1 tbsp butter over medium heat, then add shallots and a pinch of salt to the butter and stir.

2. Add vinegar and turn to medium-low. Cook 4 minutes or until vinegar has mostly evaporated.

3. Turn to low and cook 5 minutes more, then remove shallots from skillet.

4. Melt remaining butter.

5. In a blender, combine lemon juice and egg yolks with 1 tbsp water and mix until smooth.

6. Turn the blender to its lowest setting and remove the lid, then slowly drizzle in the melted butter until it has been blended into the mixture.

7. Transfer to a bowl and stir in shallots and tarragon. Season with salt and pepper to taste.

PASTA CARBONARA

While pasta dishes are primarily Italian, Swedish people have adopted them into their meals. One such dish is pasta carbonara. This is not the original Italian recipe, but a Swedish adaptation that can be altered to your tastes. Feel free to add more garlic, remove the parsley, use the entire egg instead of just the yolk and so on. Nothing can be done wrong in this recipe, as long as you enjoy the result!

INGREDIENTS

- 1 box spaghetti noodles
- ½ pound bacon
- ¼ cup heavy whipping cream 4 eggs at room temperature
- 1 cup Parmesan cheese, grated
- ¼ cup softened butter
- ¼ cup chopped fresh parsley Salt and pepper to taste

DIRECTIONS

1. Boil spaghetti according to packaging directions.

2. Cook bacon until very crisp, then let drain.

3. Beat eggs and cream together in a bowl until combined, then add Parmesan cheese, stirring gently to incorporate.

4. Add pasta to a pan or pot and toss with butter until the butter melts and coats the noodles.

5. Stir in bacon, sauce, and parsley, and mix to combine.

Serve pasta on top of spinach leaves and add a side dish of chopped tomatoes with olive oil and salt.

PANED HALIBUT FILLET WITH MASHED POTATOES

Of course, we cannot exclude fish from the menu since Swedish people eat plenty of seafood. The key to all fish is to keep it simple, like this plaice fillet . It is easy, tasty and most certainly a fail-proof dish to serve. If you can, try to get some fresh fish instead of frozen for the best flavor

INGREDIENTS

- 1 pound Halibut fillet (fresh or frozen) 1 cup breadcrumbs
- 1 large egg
- 1 pound potatoes Milk to taste Butter to taste

DIRECTIONS

1. Beat the eggs in a bowl until blended together. Set aside. Coat the plaice fillet in the egg mixture and bread it in the breadcrumbs; cover completely.

2. Fry the filet in butter in a hot skillet, about 3-5 minutes on each side. Boil the potatoes and mash them, adding milk and butter to taste. Serve the fish and mashed potatoes with a slice of lemon and a mixed salad of your choice. We recommend green peas, Brussels sprouts, broccoli, or a delicious ratatouille.

TOAST SKAGEN

This toast is more of an entree dish, and it is so delicious we could not possibly leave it out. Skagen is a place located on the Swedish west coast, but it is unclear why this particular dish was named after it. It is possibly connected with the west coast in Sweden, which is most famous for its seafood. However, this toast is a delicacy served not only in the west coast but in restaurants all over Sweden.

INGREDIENTS

- cup cooked and cooled peeled fresh shrimp 2 tsp lemon juice
- tbsp mayonnaise
- slices sourdough bread
- tbsp sour cream (or creme fraiche, if available) 2 lemon wedges
- 1 slice butter
- Dill, horseradish, and black pepper to taste

DIRECTIONS

1. Mix the shrimp with dill, horseradish, mayonnaise and sour cream, all according to your liking.
2. Season with salt, pepper, and lemon to taste.
3. Fry the bread in the butter until it is golden brown. If the bread is soaking up the butter, add more to avoid burning the bread.
4. Put the shrimp mixture on the bread. Garnish the toast with a dill, black pepper, and a lemon wedge.

These are just a few classical Swedish dishes that will make you feel satisfied without being too filling. They are delicious and easy to make with the capability to add more vegetables for added health benefits. When trying out these recipes, it is easy to understand why the Swedish have extra time to do all the things they want and need to do to achieve lagom in their lives. These recipes are simple to prepare and cook, leaving more time for enjoying free time and family.

JUNK FOOD

Junk food cannot be completely erased out of anyone's diet, even the Swedish, and we cannot write about lagom and food without mentioning junk food. Here are some tips that the Swedish use to enjoy junk food in a lagom way while still maintaining a healthy diet and lifestyle.

First and foremost, try to keep a balance. If you eat healthy and well-balanced most of the time, there is no reason why you should not enjoy junk food every once in a while. By all means, indulge yourself with a burger, some fries and a milkshake. Use the Swedish model of dining out and do it to spoil yourself instead of using fast food as a go-to everyday solution. We know that many fast food restaurants have begun serving healthier options, like carrot sticks instead of fries. But even in Sweden, fries and burgers simply cannot be separated. The healthy and conscious Swedish have figured out that if they eat healthy all the other days, they can enjoy junk food every now and then. Just don't indulge on a daily basis!

Furthermore, burgers and pizza can be made at home and are easy to prepare. Even French fries can be healthy if made at home, as the salt is controlled more than at a fast-food place. Make sure to use clean ingredients without additives or chemicals, and try to make the majority of the sauces and dough (for pizza) yourself. A homemade burger with pineapple, pickled onions, lettuce, and tomato, is not so bad. Besides, making it yourself will make you feel fuller faster and control how much you intake. Making your own fries by cutting potatoes and baking them with olive oil and salt in the oven instead of buying fries is a tastier and healthier alternative.

Making your own pizza is also a healthier option, allowing you to choose fresh ingredients and control what goes in and on your pizza. Plus, it is a fun activity for the whole family to enjoy together.

It can be overwhelming cooking at home on most nights, but it is well worth the effort. In Sweden, gathering a few friends or family and cooking together is a great way to socialize.

If you prefer having eggs in the morning, eat up. Eggs are an excellent source of protein and good fats. Plus, the Swedish eat a ton of eggs, boiled, fried, or poached, on a sandwich. They also eat scrambled eggs and bacon for breakfast at times. Keep lagom in mind and eat everything in moderations; there really are no other rules here.

PIZZA DOUGH

INGREDIENTS

- 2-½ cup flour 1 tsp sugar
- 1 tsp salt
- 1 tbsp quick-rising yeast 1 tbsp oil
- 1 cup water

DIRECTIONS

1. Combine flour, salt, sugar, and yeast in a large bowl.

2. Combine water and oil, then add to the yeast mixture.

3. Flour a cutting board or another surface, then turn the dough mixture out onto this surface.

4. Knead for two minutes.

5. Grease a bowl and place mixture into greased bowl. Cover and let stand for 20 minutes to rise.

6. Punch down dough and place onto a lined pizza pan or baking sheet. Shape into a circle or rectangle depending on the pan.

7. Bake at 400 degrees Fahrenheit for about 10 minutes.

8. Remove and top with any toppings, then bake for about 10 more minutes to complete the pizza.

9. Optionally, before baking, you can freeze or refrigerate the dough until you're ready to use it.

SNACKS

In Sweden, it is recommended to eat three larger meals and two snacks each day. This helps regulate blood sugar levels to maintain energy all day, eliminating the two o'clock crash and cravings. So, what is the Swedish snack of choice? It depends who you are asking and how old they are.

The younger children have something called a "fruit break" at school in the morning. Each child will have brought their fruit of choice in their school bag and they eat fruit together as a class. Even at home, most children are served a fruit when they crave a little something between meals. Sometimes the children are served plain yogurt along with the fruit to keep the hunger at bay a while longer if needed.

For adults, two snacks are not necessary, and most will not eat that much. The adults who do eat two snacks in-between meals will eat a fruit or plain yogurt with fruit like the children. Other common snacks are a boiled egg served with ham or another source of protein and/or a healthy sandwich. A smaller portion of the breakfast eaten as a snack or a smoothie are popular options too.The best of all is that these are all healthy and good options instead of consuming chocolate, a cookie or other sugary options. If you find yourself craving chocolate, try reaching for dark chocolate that is no lower than 70%. This is something that the Swedish indulge in every so often, but not every day. When adopting a lagom lifestyle, even when it comes to eating, the process is about finding a good balance. These changes will help you make better choices all day and in many ways. Snacking should be easy and convenient to carry and eat wherever.

When it comes to snack time, coffee is a popular choice for most Swedes. However, for those living the lagom lifestyle, it is important to not overindulge and make it a priority to find a balance. Picking the right meals for your lagom diet plan is a process that is all about balance. However, it's also important to choose foods that help you feel your best and encourage wellness at the same time. This may mean you're not eating quite as much as you're used to, or it might mean you have to rethink the types of food you reach for when you get hungry. However, making sure you choose good, quality foods and stick to the lagom principles with every bite you take can make a big difference in both your body and mind.

Picking the right food is only one aspect of eating lagom. Another important concept to keep in mind is that you should always remain balanced mentally while cooking and preparing your meals. Don't cook when you know you don't have time to complete the task, and don't overdo it by trying to prepare a recipe that sounds much too difficult for your skill level. A small challenge is always a good thing, but frustrating yourself will throw you out of the lagom mindset right away and may end up bringing some negative energies into your meal at the same time. While cooking, make sure you gather all the ingredients and tools you'll need before you get started. If you're following a recipe, keep it close at hand and take the time to double-check it to ensure your measurements are correct. This is just another way you can bring some peace and balance into your kitchen experience and give yourself a better chance at creating something successful at the same time. You may also want to make your cooking space a comfortable one by putting on some soft music in the background or opening a window for some natural air and light while you work.

When you eat, once again, give yourself time to really enjoy the process so you don't feel rushed. Chew slowly and thoughtfully, considering the flavors that are present in the food. Try each individual item on your plate separately and then try it all as one composed bite to see how the flavors and experiences change. Stop every now and then to take a drink of water so you remain hydrated, as well. You may be surprised to see just how your dining experience can change when you take time to enjoy your food!

Last but not least, plan your grocery shopping and your meals ahead of time for a better lagom experience. One of the many ways you can create balance in your life is to make sure you stay organized. Choose meals at least one week in advance and write a grocery list so you don't have to wander around the market in confusion And don't forget to always choose dishes that can be prepared with natural, healthy ingredients! Stay away from pre-packaged meals and other similar items that are not going to fit into your lagom eating.

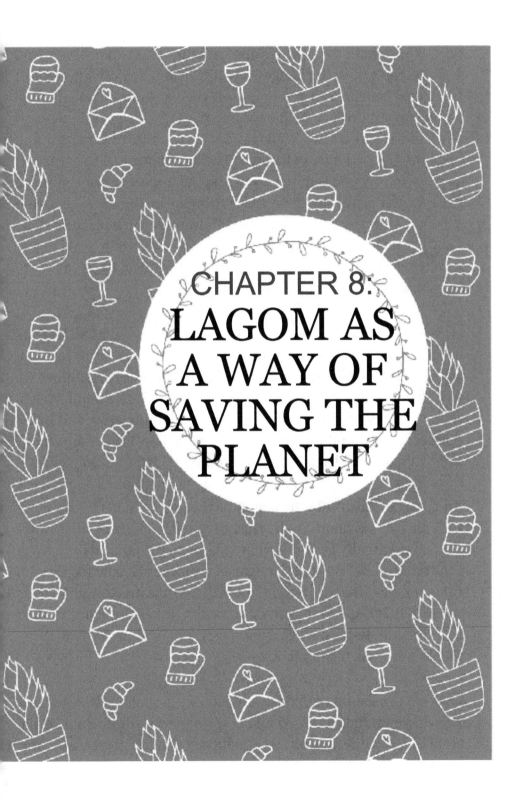

CHAPTER 8: LAGOM AS A WAY OF SAVING THE PLANET

We have covered how lagom is applied in most Swedish homes and how you can use it to change your life. The question still stands: How does the lagom lifestyle impact the world on a global level? The lagom way might help save our planet with each individual living more modest lives and, therefore, respecting nature and switching to a more green lifestyle. The lagom lifestyle suggests you are conscious of your environment and the impact your habits have on it. As you strive for doing everything in moderation, take into account how moderation can lower your impact on the planet and the environment, like decreasing pollution and damage to ecosystems from littering. In this chapter, we will discover what you can do to lead a more environmentally-friendly life.

The lagom lifestyle is closely connected to conscious habits and buying the things needed and used for functionality instead of impulse buying on a "want" basis. When we spend our money on things we were taught to believe we should want, we are being wasteful. We are told by various ads in papers, magazines, on billboards, and in TV commercials to want all sorts of different things for ourselves, our homes and our children. But, that couldn't be further from the truth.

Often, we don't consider the materials that are used in the things we buy. This includes items we buy just to sit in the closet or in a drawer that will eventually be thrown out, adding to the landfills and trash in the oceans.. By applying the lagom way in your life and focusing on building a sustainable lifestyle, you will become more aware of how money is being spent and why. Sweden is actually one of the most environmentally-friendly countries to live in, and there is much the rest of us can learn from that.

When buying something, consider not only the quality of the item but also what materials are used and how it's produced. Pick a material that will last a lifetime and is produced in an eco-conscious way.

Look for different terms on labels such as "eco," "cruelty-free" or "fair trade." There are several different labels like this, and they could vary depending on what country you live in. Read different certificates in your country or state, learn what they mean, and try to buy things that are produced that way. This will make an impact on the environment as well as the people producing them. For example, buying eco coffee means that the work environments for those working in the fields are healthier, pay is within the state or country regulations, and so on. Stay conscious of what you buy and how it affects other people. We are all not perfect, including the Swedish, but practice the lagom way often and question why you are buying things, what materials are used, and whether or not the item is sustainable for long-term usage. For example, watch out for materials in clothes that contain microplastics that wash out into the ocean during washing, or switch your ordinary coffee to an ecological brand instead. The taste will be better, and you'll be having a positive impact on the planet.

Before buying anything new, determine if you could find the same item at a thrift store or estate sale. Vintage has always been a thing in Sweden and particularly now it is a trend on the rise, where young people buy clothes and furniture from second hand shops, spending time altering the clothes or items to personalize them.

If you do buy new clothes, try to buy brands of good quality that will last throughout time. This is particularly useful for the basics in your wardrobe such as shirts, pants, jeans and so on. The Swedish prioritize a classical wardrobe so they can invest in high-quality items, rather than buying multiple cheap items that will have to be replaced each season when they become out of date.

In Sweden, many are moving to the countryside away from the hustle and bustle of the city. Although there are many new homes being built, many choose to buy older homes outside the cities and villages. Many spend their time and money restoring the homes instead of building new homes in these areas, being environmentally-conscious to how construction of new homes can affect the planet. Restoring homes can have a satisfying effect on your body and mind, and rejuvenates older homes that would have eventually been torn down.

Being environmentally-friendly and conscious, many Swedish have been growing their own plants, vegetables, and fruits in their backyards or balconies. Growing your own food is a huge trend that can save you money. Another added benefit to getting your hands dirty with Mother Nature, is that gardening can be good for the mind and soul, and can provide quality time with your family. Remember to be lagom and incorporate low maintenance plants like tomatoes, berry bushes, or flowers that require little attention and time. Growing your garden can help improve the quality of the air around you, outside and inside your home. There are many benefits to incorporating nature in your home and surroundings. While other people are stressed in the cities, making changes to incorporate nature in your life can help the planet while helping you find peace at the same time.

There are, however, many things you can do to live the lagom way and saving the planet that do not involve moving or changing your shopping habits. In Sweden, things like plastic reduction, recycling, and zero waste efforts are popular in the lagom lifestyle. As a way to minimize your impact on the planet, bring reusable bags to the supermarket, buy sustainable, quality clothes, and minimize your waste. Also, the Swedish people love to recycle almost everything such as plastic, paper, glass bottles,tin cans, and so on.

CHAPTER 9:
LAGOM CLOTHING

When you're working on your lagom lifestyle, there's no reason why you can't include your wardrobe in the process, too. Your clothes can showcase lagom just like every other part of your life ,if you know how to make them work for you. However, picking clothes that are lagom can be a little tricky, so be sure to take your time when doing this. Don't go overboard, and really stop to consider your purchases before making them. Remember, not too little and not too much is the way to go when you're shopping for lagom clothing items! Here are a few more tips to keep in mind:

- Balance, balance, balance. Remember that keeping lagom is all about making sure you don't swing too far in one direction or the other. This means that you shouldn't go wild with tons of different vibrant colors and strange styles, but it also means you don't have to feel like you're wearing a boring, drab outfit every time you step out of the house, either. Look for something that bridges the gap between both of these concepts and helps you look good without drawing an unnecessary amount of attention to the clothing at the same time.

- Function over form. The clothes you choose for a lagom wardrobe should be functional—and comfortable! You shouldn't be worried about how you look to others, but should instead focus on how the clothing works for you and how it makes you feel.

Always choose something comfortable and easy to move around in. You don't have to wear something that restricts your movement or is made of fabric you can barely stand to touch. You don't even have to wear uncomfortable shoes just because they look good!

- Pick items that are made to last and won't cost a fortune. You don't have to pay hundreds of dollars for a high-quality pair of pants when you can find a comparable item for fifty dollars or less. On the other hand, buying a pair of pants that's only twenty dollars but will wear out in less than a year of use isn't very good balance, either. Look for something middle-of-the-road that's made of durable materials but isn't on the high end of the pricing scale.

- Saving money and keeping things minimalistic is the most important factor in choosing clothes for your lagom wardrobe.. Be frugal and don't worry about stocking up on name brand items when an off-brand will work just as well for the same situations.

- Sustainability is important. One of the key facets of lagom involves making sustainable, green, eco-friendly decisions to help improve balance on a global scale choose clothes that are made from sustainable materials or produced in factories that don't contribute as much to pollution as others do. It may be tough to find these brands, but they're out there, and supporting them can make a big difference .

- Upcycle or recycle your clothes when possible. Turn them into something new or use worn out clothes for cleaning rags. Donate clothes that are still in good condition to local thrift stores and shelters, or ask members of your family if they can use them instead. Don't just throw them away!

- Last but not least, don't neglect spring cleaning for your lagom wardrobe! Once a year, go through your clothes and consider each item. If you haven't worn the item within the last year—during the correct season when you might've done so—then it's time to get rid of it. Even if you love it and feel like you're sure to wear it again in the future, just take a deep breath and donate or throw it out. Chances are good that, if the item didn't come into your mind as an option during the past year, that is not going to change in the coming year either.

Clothing is one of the many areas people tend to gloss over when they're planning their lagom lives. While clothing is one of the central concepts in hygge, it may not be the first thing on your mind when you're thinking of practicing lagom. There are several tips you can keep in mind when learning how to lagom your wardrobe, however, so take your time working through these concepts to help you get a better idea of what to expect from this overhaul. Be ready to get rid of some items and understand that you may not be buying new ones to replace those items as you go through this list.

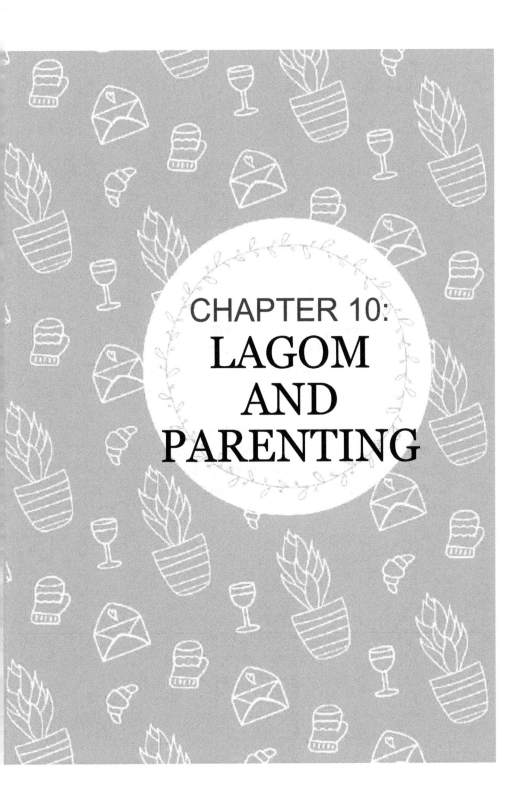

CHAPTER 10:
LAGOM AND PARENTING

Did you know you can even apply the concept of lagom to your experience as a parent? Although parenting is a very personal matter and varies from family to family, many parents choose to incorporate lagom beliefs and elements into the way they raise their children. Perhaps not surprisingly, a lot of these ideas come from the way families in Sweden raise their children as well, and these concepts are becoming popularized throughout the rest of the world If you're interested in giving this a try, you should keep in mind the following suggestions:

- Let in some natural light—and natural air, too. Especially when your child is still a baby, consider opening the window to let in some light and air while your little one is napping. In Sweden, many doctors even recommend doing this to encourage the growth of a healthy immune system. Of course, if your baby has any health risks that could be aggravated by this, it's best to skip this suggestion and pick something else from the list of lagom parenting options. If not, however, don't be afraid to let your child breathe in some nature now and then!

- Spend as much time with your children as you can, but remember balance is key. Families in Sweden spend time together often and even take long, extended vacations together as well. Swedish parents play outdoors with their children and care about what's going on in their children's lives, too. On the other hand, it's important to keep things balanced and in check, and remember that your child is an individual. Children need their own private time away from parents and other family members sometimes, too, so respect your kids' boundaries while still making sure to spend time with them.

- Remember that it's okay to use childcare. In Sweden, parents tend to send their children to a childcare facility from an early age, and it's not frowned upon to do this when you need to get back to work after having a baby. Swedish daycares come in many variations and there are plenty of options out there for families to choose from. But keep in mind, too, that if you send your child to a daycare, you should set aside some time to spend one-on-one (or as a family unit) with your little one every single day to make sure all of their emotional needs are being met.

For a true lagom lifestyle, children should be encouraged to play outdoors. Parents should also get involved and should either be active with their children while outside or should remain close by while children play. This is for safety as well as for the benefit of the whole family emotionally! Playing outside, getting active, and having plenty of access to fresh air and sunshine is an important part of the lagom life all year long. In Sweden, many families send their children out to play whether it's warm, cold, raining, or snowing.

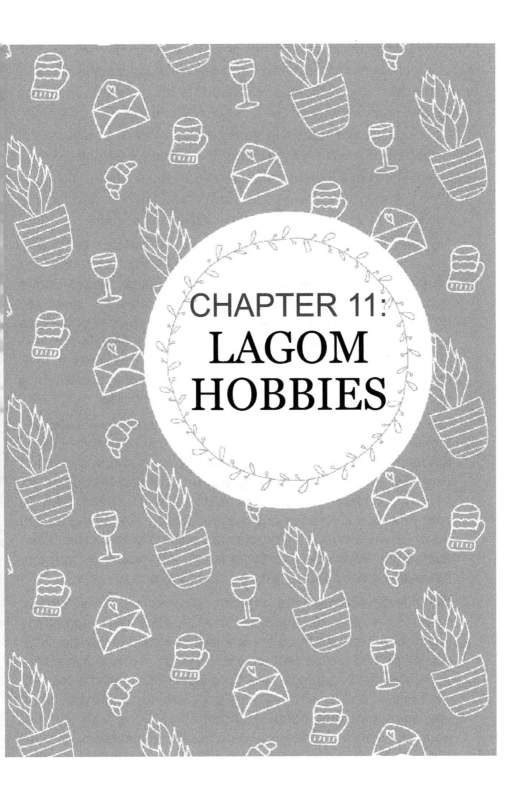

CHAPTER 11: LAGOM HOBBIES

Are you interested in finding out how to keep lagom close to your heart even when enjoying your hobbies? While you're relaxing and enjoying the things that make you happy in life, you can remember lagom and work to achieve the balance you crave at the same time. You may even decide to take up some new hobbies that can be lagom, too, especially if you feel a little bit adrift without something to spend your free time on. Remember that lagom is about finding the right balance between work, time with family and friends, and time to yourself as well, and hobbies are an integral part of that!

- No matter what your hobby is, keep things in balance every time you enjoy it. You may be tempted to spend all your free time on your hobby, but remember that you should choose varied activities to create a true balanced lagom lifestyle. However, don't neglect to give yourself plenty of time to enjoy your hobbies as well. And if possible, consider bringing the people you love into your hobby, too, by showing them what you're working on or encouraging them to learn about it as well. When you share a hobby, you're enjoying even more lagom in your life.

- Don't let your work become your hobby. Many people—especially those who own their own business or work from home—have a tendency to let work and hobby time become one in the same. A hobby should be something you enjoy doing that does not cause you stress. If your hobby is bringing you stress, then it's time to take a step back and maybe look for something else to do while you emotionally process the source of the issue. It can sometimes be impossible to do this if your hobby is your job, however, so keep these two separate from one another.

- Don't underestimate the importance of some of the classic relaxation hobbies out there. You may be interested in something much different, but if you try one of these old familiar hobbies, you might find it's perfect for you after all. Try woodworking if you enjoy building things, take up painting or drawing if you feel like being creative, or opt for knitting, sewing, or crochet when you enjoy having a hobby you can bring along with you just about anywhere. These may seem like old-fashioned or "boring" choices, but they can make a big difference in a lagom life.

Remember to remain frugal and don't overspend on your hobby. Yes, you might have a pricey hobby—such as classic cars, for example —but you should still make sure to create a budget and stick to it when making purchases related to this part of your life. You probably don't need every hobby-related item you think about purchasing, and therefore it's a good idea to write these items down, wait a day or two, and then see how you feel about buying them. Chances are good you'll realize they're not all necessary, and you'll be able to spend your money only on those items required to enjoy your hobby instead.

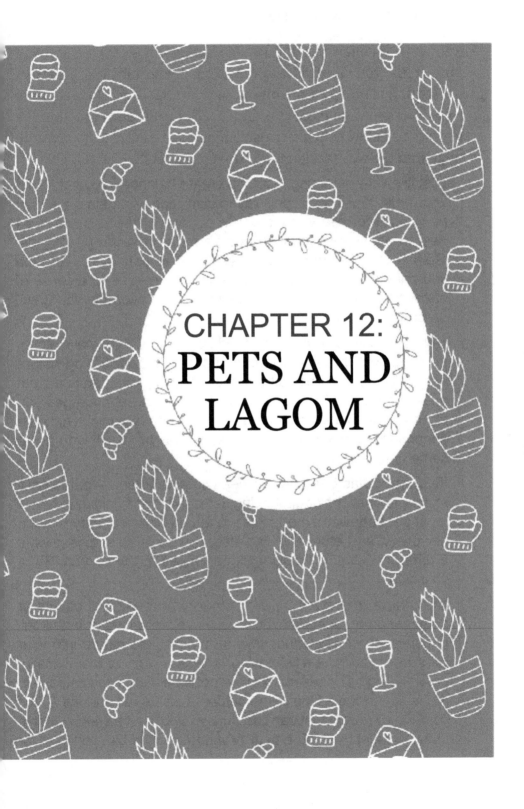

CHAPTER 12:
PETS AND LAGOM

Even when it comes to the furry (or feathery or scaly) members of your family, you can find ways to bring lagom into your life, too. Pets tend to bring joy more often than not, but they can also bring stress now and then too. Keep this in mind while you check out the suggestions below to help you determine the best way to incorporate lagom into the way you keep and treat your pets.

- Just like with parenting, you can create balance in your life with your pets, too. The proper way to discipline and train a pet may be difficult for everyone to agree on, but for the most part, it's best to practice rewarding good behavior in your furry friends. Getting into this habit from day one with your pets can help you balance their behavior and may even help bring a sense of calm to the whole household that will carry over into your pets' personalities, too.

- Get out and enjoy nature together! Particularly if you have a dog, don't neglect the time you can spend outside enjoying nature and getting some fresh air together. Walking your dog is a great activity for you, since it gets you outside and encourages you to be active. But it's also great for your dog, who will enjoy the chance to burn off some energy as well as bond with you at the same time.

- If your dog has been having behavioral problems—particularly related to chewing or destroying items that don't belong to him—most pet behavioral therapists will encourage you to try walking him every day before anything else. You might be surprised what a difference a short daily walk can make in the personality of your pup!

- If you have an indoor cat or another type of pet that cannot or does not go outdoors—even if you have a hamster or a tank full of fish—you can still find ways to bring a little nature into your pet's life. If you have a fish tank or a terrarium with a lizard, snake, or turtle living in it, research some pet-safe plants you can use in the tank to bring a little of the outdoors inside to your pet. And if you have a rodent that can't go outside and can't have real plants either, try just opening a nearby window a little bit every day for some fresh air. Just be careful not to do this when it could be too chilly for your pet or if it could allow a predator to get inside!

Practice balance when choosing whether or not to bring home new pets, too. You may be an animal lover and might want to bring home every stray or needy animal you see. However, this habit is not lagom, and it's not going to bring you balance. Instead, it may cause you a lot of stress as your home becomes cluttered, destroyed, and overrun with pets. Take this into consideration as you carefully choose which pets are right for you and the other people in your household, too.

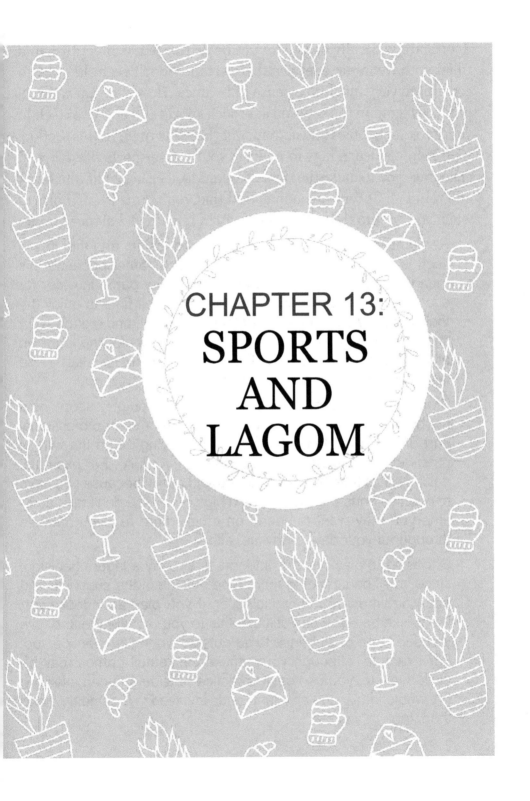

CHAPTER 13:
SPORTS AND LAGOM

Sports are generally considered to be fast-paced, competitive, and filled with dynamic energies that certainly don't seem like they'd contribute very much to a sense of balance. However, you can still practice lagom in the way you approach sports and enjoy yourself in your favorite hobbies and activities at the same time. In this section, we'll help you learn how to manage your active sports lifestyle and encourage you to make the right decisions to keep lagom in your heart and mind at all times. You may find that your game even improves when you go into the competition with a refreshed, balanced mind.

- Remember that life is full of winning and losing, and that this in itself is a balance. You cannot win every game, because this means someone else would be losing every game in order for everything to balance out. Everyone has their time to enjoy the thrill of victory as well as the sadness of defeat, and a good sport should be happy for the other team even while feeling let down about losing. Understanding this concept can make it feel a little less disappointing when this ends up happening to you.

- Practicing your game is important, whether you play sports as a hobby or you make it a more professional or semi-professional part of your life. However, don't let practicing get in the way of other activities you need to attend to in your life. For example, don't neglect time with your friends and family because you have to practice constantly for the next big game. And don't take away time you may want to spend on other, more relaxing hobbies throughout your day-to-day life, either.

- Choosing to play a sport outdoors is already a lagom decision, since you'll be spending more time outside in the sunshine and fresh air when you play. However, if you play an indoor sport like basketball, you can still use this to your advantage and give yourself more of a chance to go outside when you practice, too. For example, although your official basketball games may be played inside, you can easily practice outside and can even get the whole family and all your friends involved in a game now and then, too.

Don't forget to involve your kids in your sports lifestyle whenever possible! Kids may not be interested in more complicated adult sports like golf (although they might be more interested than you may expect), but they're likely to want to join in if you're playing soccer or softball in the backyard. These games may not be full sporting events, but they are a great way to teach your children healthy exercise habits, good sportsmanship, and the best way to remain lagom throughout every aspect of their lives, too. You can even use a family game to teach your children how to play a new sport, which can bring more balance to their lives as well. You never know when you might be teaching your child their new favorite hobby!

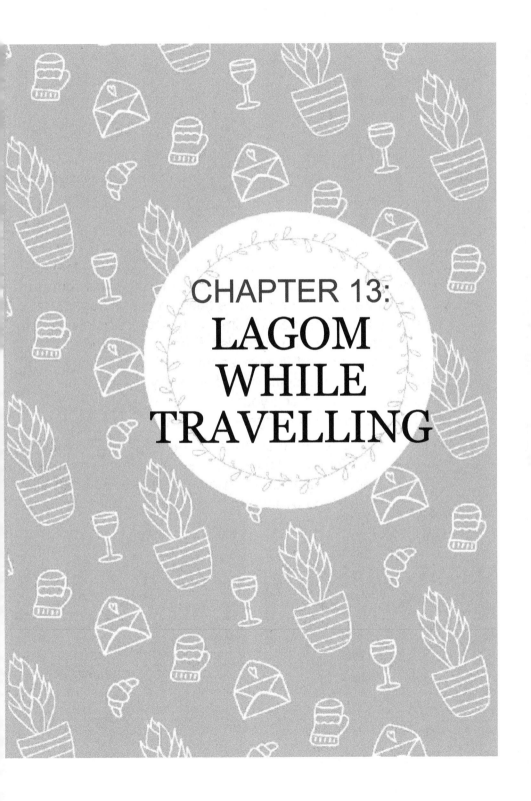

CHAPTER 13:
LAGOM WHILE TRAVELLING

Taking a vacation from work can be an extremely relaxing experience. On the other hand, planning and executing a vacation—especially to a location you've never visited before—can be extremely stressful. Traveling may also be a strenuous time for you and your whole family, even though it's supposed to be a chance to have some fun and bond together. Practicing lagom throughout your travels and the whole time you're on vacation can help you stay focused, relaxed, and mindful of everything going on around you, and it can even help you form stronger, longer-lasting memories of the experience, too. Here are a few tips to help you get started.

- Make plans, but don't stress about sticking to them word-for-word. For example, you should definitely make plans when it comes to scheduling transportation such as taking a plane, bus, or train. You should also plan ahead of time and choose a hotel near the destinations you're planning to visit. From there, however, try to keep things loose and flexible so you don't feel bogged down trying to stick to a specific schedule every day. And don't be afraid to give yourself and your family some downtime to enjoy your hotel room or just lounge around by the pool, too.

- When traveling to another country, take the opportunity to bond with your family by learning some key words and phrases together in another language while you're there. You can also create memories and bonding experiences by trying new foods and visiting important landmarks.

- Always practice balance and be respectful when visiting cultures outside your own. You may not understand why a culture partakes in a certain practice, eats a certain food, or celebrates a certain holiday, but you can still be respectful and take the chance to learn a little more at the same time. You may be able to expand your worldview considerably when you do this, and in turn, you might find a new level of balance in your heart and mind, too.

- If you'll be traveling to a hectic destination, like a major theme park or a busy beach, encourage everyone in the family to take some quiet time in which they can nap, read a book, learn about the surrounding area, or listen quietly to a favorite album. Even if this quiet time only lasts an hour, it can provide a valuable reset in the middle of a busy and sometimes overwhelming day.

Never be afraid to take a vacation that's really just for relaxing. You may feel like you need to plan lots of activities, especially if you have younger kids in your family or are traveling with a big group. However, you shouldn't underestimate how vital it can be to just get together and have fun with some different scenery for a little while. Consider renting a large cabin in the mountains together with your extended family and spending that time cooking outdoors, fishing, hiking, and enjoying nature. This is just one example of a true lagom vacation experience.

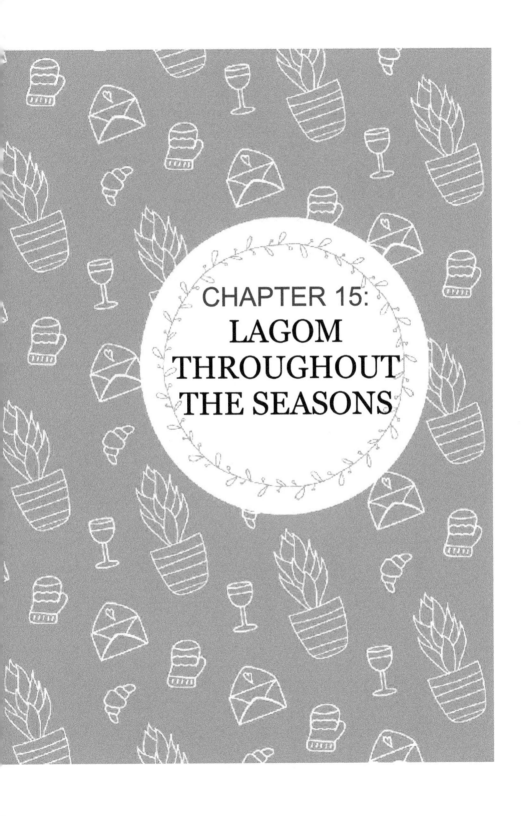

CHAPTER 15:
LAGOM THROUGHOUT THE SEASONS

As the seasons change, the way you approach lagom will change as well. However, just because the year is progressing that doesn't mean you should neglect lagom at any point. The changing of the seasons and the celebration of various holidays can help remind you of what balance truly is and can help you keep a positive frame of mind when thinking about this balance, too.

Remember that tentir world and everyone living on the planet is balanced by time. We all experience time the same way, and this can provide a sense of peace and mindfulness to anyone who stops to think about it. Time may bring about changes, but those changes are just another way the planet balances itself. Even as different weather patterns approach throughout the changing seasons, this, too, is the planet working to maintain the perfect balance it needs to continue spinning through space in just the right way.

There are several ways you can keep lagom in your mind and heart throughout the seasons. In this section, you'll find suggestions to help you maintain balance and peace in your life no matter what time of year it might be. It can be helpful to refer to this list when you feel a little lost or adrift at certain points throughout the year, so keep it handy when you need a quick refresher to help you on your path to lagom.

SPRING

- Spring is a time of balance, when new life is blooming and growing outdoors and changes are likely to be made in many aspects of your own existence too. As the world wakes up again after the cold of winter, this is an excellent time to reflect on the meaning of balance in your life and what you can do to improve the sense of peace you experience when you practice lagom.

- In the spring, focus on cleaning and refreshing your living space for the coming year. This is a great time to go through your wardrobe and check it for any items you might not be wearing anymore. If they're still in good shape, donate them; if not, try to repurpose them in some way by adding them to a rag pile or gathering fabric for crafting.

- This is a great time clean the floors, windows, and other often-neglected parts of your home as well. Take time to really get into every corner when you do your spring cleaning and your home will be ready for the coming year in no time.

- Consider re-organizing your work space if you have an office job or something similar, too. There may be ways to make your job more efficient that you haven't even considered before, and you might be surprised at what a difference a little organization and change of scenery at the workplace can make, too.

- Take time during the spring to think of ways you can get involved with outdoor activities. Although it may not be quite warm enough yet to go outside often, depending on where you live, this is a good time to start branching out and encouraging kids to play outside longer in the evenings as the days lengthen, too.

- If you're thinking of getting a new pet, this can be a nice time of year to do so. Getting a pet in the spring gives your family time to get to know this new addition before summer rolls around and the kids will be home from school. However, don't get a pet if you're not financially, mentally, and physically prepared to take care of it, as this may throw off your balance and negatively impact the lagom in your household instead.

SUMMER

- In the summertime, plan to spend much more time outdoors, preferably engaging in physical activities with the whole family. This is the best time of year to play sports or to enjoy hiking, biking, swimming, and many other outdoor hobbies. Teach your children to exercise and get lots of fresh air during the summertime. And don't be afraid to spend some of that time relaxing and having a meal with your family, too!

- Since school is out during the summer, make plans to travel and take a vacation with your family. Remember the tips in the Travel chapter earlier in this book to help you make the most of your vacation experience while sticking to your lagom lifestyle. Keep in mind that over-stressing about your vacation isn't going to be relaxing for anyone involved, so you may be better off planning a small "staycation," especially if you don't have the money in your budget for something more extensive.

- Summer is a great time to try new recipes and learn something about cooking, too. This is the time of year when many families get together at least once, and sometimes a lot more often than that, to share meals and have fun with each other. If you're getting together with your extended family, why not take the opportunity to learn to make something new? You might even want to share that experience with family members you don't see often, like favorite cousins, aunts, or uncles.

- Let your hobbies shine during the summer, when you have more time to focus on fun. Whatever your hobby might be, this is a great time to learn something new about it. Strike a balance in your life by giving yourself time to work on your hobbies without overdoing it, and make sure you're still taking care of your family and work needs at the same time. You might even consider learning an entirely new hobby during the summer months!

FALL

- This cozy time of the year is the best time to start practicing your hygge, but there's no reason why you can't do a little lagom improvement during the fall, too. Try working on the way you balance your "me time" with your work and family time during the fall season. Set aside more opportunities for a little quiet time to yourself as the weather starts to get a little cooler.

- The nights will be getting longer at this time of the year, so why not consider a few more activities that you can enjoy after the sun goes down? You may want to sit outside and chat with your friends and family in the cooler night air during the fall, since insects won't be as prominent and the temperature may be more comfortable. This is a good time to reconnect with friends you might have lost touch with during the hectic summer months, too.

- Take time in the fall to pamper yourself. Give yourself one night a week, if you can, to take a long bubble bath and enjoy the time alone without the stressors of the rest of your life. Restore balance in your heart and mind by lighting some aromatherapy candles, putting on some soft music, and maybe having a small glass of wine or some caffeine-free tea to help you wind down after a busy work day.

- During the fall, you may plan big, hearty meals with your family and possibly with your friends as well. This can be an excellent way to bring balance to your family life, but make sure you set aside the time it takes to prepare these meals and enjoy them without pushing yourself beyond your limits emotionally.

WINTER

- Many family-oriented holidays occur during the winter months, so keep this in mind when working on your lagom lifestyle. This is a time of year when families get together a lot more often and share experiences with one another, but it can also be stressful for those who plan these gatherings. If you're going to be doing a lot of cooking or other planning for your extended family, don't forget to take time for yourself too. This is especially crucial during the holidays.

- Try decorating in a lagom way for the holiday season. It can be tempting to throw a lot of lots and sparkly garland around your home, but this isn't really a balanced way to decorate. Keep things simple, minimalistic, but effective. Stick to silver and gold or opt for white lights instead of rainbow-colored ones. Light candles to create mood and ambience, and play soft background music rather than letting loud holiday movies blast on the television all day long.

- If you have children, encourage them to understand that less can be more. During the holiday season, kids end up wanting a lot of new toys and other items thanks to the commercialization of many holidays. This can be a teaching moment for you and your family to learn a little about what it means to get something of value, and to help your children understand the concept of quality over quantity.

- Once you figure out the best way to keep lagom going all year long, you'll be able to put these concepts into practice year after year. With more experience, you'll be better able to remember how you incorporated the practice into your life from the previous year and be more prepared to face whatever may come your way.

CHAPTER 16:
21-DAY LAGOM CHALLENGE

We will wrap this book up with twenty-one different challenges to give the Swedish lifestyle a chance and find out if it is a fit for you. Challenge yourself to adopt the lagom lifestyle and have an open mind. Be sure to track your progress in a journal during 21 days to see what works for you and your family. Some of the challenges will seem huge and need more time than just a day to adjust, but choose a small area of your life or home to change and narrow it down little by little. Once you feel confident with a change, continue on with another change until the lagom lifestyle is achieved.

Here's a list to help aid you on your way to achieving the lagom way:

1. KITCHEN AND DINING ROOM

Instead of attending or hosting a party, meet up with your closest friends and have some hygge time. This might include something simple as a good cup of coffee at a local coffee shop or having a simple dinner at home. The possibilities are endless.

2. SELF-CARE

Schedule some alone time today and do something that recharges your batteries. It could be a walk in the forest or a trail, a bubble bath, or staying in bed reading a book for a while in the morning or in the evening. The key is to find tranquility with yourself.

3. SPEND TIME IN NATURE

Get outside and enjoy what's around you. Take a walk, ride your bike, or do anything to get you moving. Spending time close to nature is good for your body and soul.

4. TRY SOMETHING NEW

Why not try a new hobby today? Do something you don't think you'll enjoy doing. You might be surprised. Or, do something that you are afraid of doing, like skydiving or going to a new town to explore. If you feel uncomfortable doing it yourself, bring a friend.

5. TAKE UP AN OLD HOBBY

Rekindle those old hobbies you use to enjoy. Sometimes we quit doing things without even knowing why when life gets too busy. This will help find peace and tranquility with yourself and your life.

6. SAY NO

Today's challenge is to say no to something. The Swedish are people pleasers, but they are willing to say no to things they don't have the time for or feel like doing. Say no to something today, and you'll be surprised at how calm you may feel afterward. Remember, you can't do everything every time for everyone.

7. SETTLE FOR GOOD ENOUGH

If you are a perfectionist, this will be hard. Sometime today, when you are performing a task, challenge yourself to leave your task once it is done. If you have done it properly, consider it done if it is good enough even if you don't find it perfect. Try it and see what happens. If you don't feel comfortable doing this at work, try at home. When cleaning, settle when it is clean even if there still might be some little thing left to clean. Don't overexert yourself to accomplish perfection each time. No one will probably notice the small imperfection anyway.

8. DECLUTTER YOUR HOME

Choose a room or small space to start the decluttering process. Do not take on your whole home as it will become overwhelming and discouraging. Tackle a drawer, a cupboard, or closet first, or even your desk, to declutter and open up space. Ask yourself questions to assess in the decluttering process:

- Do I use this item on a regular basis?
- Do I need this item (if yes, make sure you know what you need
- it for)?
- Do I love this item?
- Do I need more of this? (Ask this question if you already have multiple similar items.)

Only keep the things you use and need. Not all items are useful; some are only decorations and can stay as long as you like the item and as long as it has a given place.

Once you are done, organize what is left and get rid of the clutter through donation or reselling.

9. DECLUTTER AND ORGANIZE YOUR WARDROBE

Go through your closet and get rid of the things you no longer use or like. Instead of throwing them out, donate them or sell online. After you have decided what will stay, go ahead and organize your wardrobe, so it is easy to find everything. If this challenge seems too hard or becomes overwhelming, narrow it down. Choose one area to begin with, like cleaning out your underwear drawer and organizing it properly. Then continue on with the rest another day.

10. CHOOSE OUTFITS FOR A WEEK AHEAD

Organizing your clothes is one step. Today, plan out your outfits for the week ahead and stick to them. If this seems overwhelming, plan a few days ahead until it becomes a habit you enjoy doing. Planning outfits in advance can save time and energy in the morning. Your clothes are put together already, making getting dressed easy and efficient in the morning.

11. GO VINTAGE SHOPPING

Shopping at thrift stores and online second hand retailers helps recycle old clothes and adds personality to your wardrobe and home with unique and one-of-a-kind items. If you don't find the perfect use of your imagination and see if you can find something that is easy to alter and incorporate it in your home or wardrobe.

12. EXERCISE OUTSIDE

Leave the gym and take your exercise outside. Take in the fresh air and all the benefits of being outdoors. You don't need much equipment or special workout clothes. Lace up your running shoes, throw on comfortable clothes, and go for a brisk walk or run. Feel the need for some strength training? Stop and do pushups and sit-ups, or do them once you get home.

13. SWITCH SIDES

If you are usually active and social, try a mindful and calm exercise like yoga or meditation. If you are more of yoga and meditating kind of person, then try an intense and social activity like a spinning class or dance class. While mixing up your workouts will help maintain your body, it's a perfect way to find a balance between being social and being in solitude while finding the lagom way in your exercise routine.

14. PLAN OUT MEALS FOR ONE WEEK AHEAD

Write a meal plan for a week for breakfast, lunch, and dinner, and stick to that shopping list and menu. Make the plan according to your taste and circumstances and put it in writing so you will not forget it. If you want more of a challenge, choose dishes with similar ingredients so that you don't have to buy as many items at the grocery store. You can buy less and make sure to use all the food you buy, so you don't have to throw anything away.

15. WRITE A SHOPPING LIST AND STICK TO IT

Write a shopping list and stick to it at the grocery store. Don't forget to buy other essential items such as toilet paper, detergent and so on. This will help you save time, money, and the energy not to go back to the grocery store multiple times in the week. The more often you go shopping during the week, the more likely you are to impulse buy.

16. SWEDISH COOKING

Instead of going out for dinner, try cooking for yourself and eat at home. If you don't have a family who is eating with you, invite a few friends to keep you company. Try a Swedish dish included in this book. If you want to challenge yourself further, make extra food and bring the leftovers to work for lunch the next day and save some money.

17. PACK A SNACK

Try out a healthy snack instead of coffee and chocolate this afternoon. Prepare a nice and simple snack, like a fruit or a healthy sandwich, to eat when you feel those afternoon cravings kicking in.

18. DIY JUNK FOOD

Gather with your family or friends and cook your own junk food. Make pizza or maybe fries and burgers. The choice is yours. Find a recipe you like and just do it. Eat and enjoy.

19. RECYCLE YOUR GARBAGE

Gather your trash and recycle it. The Swedish do it all the time. Recycle everything from paper to plastic, and clothes. It is all according to the lagom way, and part of environmentally responsible lifestyle.

20. EDUCATE YOURSELF

The Swedish apply a lagom approach to their shopping habits and how they buy things because they read about products that are earth-friendly. So today, read up on environmental-friendly and/or cruelty-free labels. Consider switching over to these brands as they are more sustainable options, which is better for the planet.

21. SWITCH TO A FRIENDLIER OPTION

Try to use eco, fair trade or cruelty-free products instead of fast and cheaply made items. For example, if you are buying new facial products see if you can find an eco-friendly choice or buy ecological fruits the next time you visit the grocery store. Another thing you can do is try to find locally produced products to buy. When buying locally, you are supporting your community. Farmers and small business people will love you for it.

CONCLUSION

Now that you've had a chance to read through this book, you should have some ideas of what to expect when you give lagom a try. You may be able to more clearly define the goals you want to set out for yourself, and you'll be prepared with suggestions to back you up every step of the way. You may have even learned more about lagom than you ever thought possible!

Take your time considering how you want to implement the concept of lagom into your daily life. From there, you can use the information in this book to guide you as you bring lagom into your home and your heart. Good luck, and remember: balance is key!

Thank you!

REVIEWS

Reviews and feedback help improve this book and the author. If you enjoy this book, we would greatly appreciate it if you could take a few moments to share your opinion and post a review on Amazon.

FREE BONUS

HYGGE GIFT IDEAS

Go to https://mailchi.mp/752b5b4dd620/mayathoresen to download the guide for free